Dedication

Dedicated to the loving memory of my Grandmother, Carrie Davis, who gave her all to help her children, grandchildren, and great-grandchildren grow. To my wife, Erica, for her unparalleled love, support, and friendship.

Acknowledgments

The Universal Oneness, My Mother; Margaret Jean Burton-Day. My Wife; Erica Inez Moore. My Grandmother; Carrie Davis and My Sisters; Chivette & Abika. Omar, Matt, Uncle Tommy, Kenny, Neese, Clarence, Ernie, Samara, Marlene, Bettie Jean, Uncle Omar, Uncle Pete, Dayvon, Michael, Jordan, Billy Burton & family, Arthur Day, LaCretia Day, Maryse Weekes, Coach Ron Graham, Nancy Carlson, Melody Prunty, Mr. Hamilton, Rodney & The Carter family, Coach Steve Lewis, Cornell S. Brown, Jr., Roger Kingdom, Sam Woodhouse III, Paul Bennett, Derrick Headen, Justin Laing & family, Louis Jefferson, Henry Jefferson, Paul Leonard, Larry Meadows Jr., Maurice Walcot, Mike Bygraves, Tommy Rice, Femi, Abe, Kim Reddick, Martine Cadet, Sybil Berry, Alverta Berry, Tony Sabatino, Joel Hayes, Mark Deville, Nicole McDargh & Carrie Mitchell, Zeena, Michelle Lambert, Thurman Matthiesen, John Murchison, Dr. Vernell Lillie, Dayna Hamlin, Trevor & Margaret Moore, Claudine, Alicia, Shaline, Liani & Dale, Bruce Barnes, Mrs. Smith, Russell G. Jones, Nilaja Sun, Russell Hornsby, Danny Simmons, Beresford Bennett, Mustafa Effortless, Alan Laws, Porter Strudwick, Rhea Lewis, Denise Shelton, Monique Ruffin, Heather Maybin, Kelly Wood, Allie, Trudy & Amir Baylock, Meski, Kassa & Menelik, Kareem Ferguson, Mark Ewing, The Regis Family, Robert Fonte, Leslie Horne, Nancy Washington, John Fahy, Alexis Archer, Philip Thompson, Allison Williams, Harold Surratt, David Reinhardt, Gina Williams, Dygretta Watson, Omari Shariff, Antonio Lyons, Way Deep, Raymond Floyd, Louise Gaillard. Jamestown, Chicago, Pittsburgh, Brooklyn, Los Angeles, Denver, London. Omega Psi Phi, Gamma Mu, Iota Phi, Bay Cities Toastmasters, Century City Toastmasters, CapoeiraBrasil, Chautauqua Region Community Foundation & Chautauqua Striders

Thank you also to my virtual mentors, Muhammad Ali, Bruce Lee, Oprah Winfrey, Richard Branson, Robin Sharma, Donald Trump, Brian Tracy, Les Brown, OSHO, Tony Robbins, Bob Marley, KRS One, James Allen, John Alston, Neville Goodard, Wayne Dyer, Deepak Chopra, Bob Proctor, Paul Scheele and Paul McKenna.

My entire family and all my friends.

This list is definitely a starting point and in no way all inclusive. I thank those that I was unable to mention.

Table of Contents

Preface

You have the power to choose happiness now!
In this book you will learn solid ideas and methods that I, and many others, have used to finally achieve a successful and happy life. Many times, happiness is simply a matter of changing your perspective.

The sentiments and actions that I would like to inspire with this book are exemplified by the following quote:

"To laugh often and love much; to win the respect of intelligent persons and the affection of children; to earn the approbation of honest critics; to appreciate beauty; to give of one's self, to leave the world a bit better, whether by a healthy child, a garden patch or a redeemed social condition; to have played and laughed with enthusiasm and sung with exultation; to know even one life has breathed easier because you have lived—that is to have succeeded."
- Ralph Waldo Emerson

This book will provide you with practical techniques that you can start implementing today. You will be exposed to tools that can condition your mind so that happiness becomes the easy choice.

These principles have been tried and tested many times over, and they only work when you invest the time and energy into acting on them. Life is to be experienced, so live and love fully.

Choose happiness now!

HOW TO CHOOSE
HAPPINESS...MOST OF THE TIME:
30 WAYS IN 30 DAYS

Take a moment right now to assess your life. At this point in time, are you interested in experiencing more **joy** and **happiness**? If so, this book will provide you with ideas that will work wonders in your life. But they will only work if you apply yourself and truly commit to the process of choosing your actions and attitudes.

This is a "play-along-with-me" book that calls for your active participation. Inside are many exercises, principles, and tools, but these tools are no good to you if you do not put them to use. You are going to get out what you put into this. Reading and reflecting on these principles and stories is one part of the process; having fun and doing the exercises is the other.

I'm excited that you've invested your money, and more importantly your time into developing yourself into a more successful, happier person. In my early life I experienced many difficulties; therefore I know what it's like to be very unhappy.

I was abused as a child, and at a very young age I witnessed the tragic murder of my step-father and biological mother while playing on the playground in Chicago, IL.

I'll go into a bit more detail about this situation later in the book, but in short, I have forgiven the assailant and dedicated my life to sharing the tools and techniques that I used to overcome the would-be negative effects that these events could have had on my life then and now. In this book I will share all of the secrets—which I have picked up over the past twenty years—to living a successful and happy life.

Today, I am in a wonderful relationship, I am successfully living my dream of having a positive impact on others, and I am grateful to currently be in excellent health. In this book you will learn how to achieve your own definition of success and happiness.

Whether you are new to self-development programs, or a self-help junkie like me, I invite you to experience the ideas in this book with an open mind and an open heart. More importantly, I encourage you to take action and perform the steps outlined in each section.

This book is laid out as follows:
1. 4 Steps to Getting Anything You Want
2. 6 Principles for Attaining Joy and Fulfillment In Your Life S.M.I.L.E.S.
3. Ruminations: My Personal Journey So Far
4. 30 Ways in 30 Days with 30 Action Steps to Help Make Happiness a Habit

This book is your "portable work shop." Read it through first and then go back and perform the action steps in the order that suits your lifestyle. As your personal coach and cheerleader I am going to challenge you to step outside of your comfort zone. I'm going to challenge you to commit yourself, and I'm going to challenge you to participate fully. So, whether it takes 30 days, 30 weeks, or longer, be sure to complete this book, including all of the action steps provided.

I am going to share my personal stories with you, including some things that my closest friends don't even know about me. I'm going to allow myself to be vulnerable and I am going to give you 100%, so let's take this journey together. Many have used and continue to use these tools to get more out of life, myself included. We have achieved better health, greater success, and more happiness; you can too. You just have to read on, do the exercises, be flexible, and keep taking productive actions towards your goals.

What is Happiness Exactly?

Let's start with a definition of "Happiness." This definition is from the online Encyclopedia Wikipedia:

Happiness is an emotional or effective state that is characterized by feelings of enjoyment, pleasure, and satisfaction. As a state and as a subject it has been pursued and commented on extensively throughout world history. This reflects the universal importance that humans place on happiness. Other states associated with happiness include well-being, delight, inner-peace, health, safety, contentment, and love. Contrasting states include suffering, depression, grief, anxiety, and pain.

Before I go any further, I want to let you know that I define myself as a "spiritual being having a human experience." Being human means that I allow myself to experience a wide range of emotions. I want to make it perfectly clear that I am not happy 100% of the time. If you're looking for a book that will make you happy all of the time, then this book is not for you!

What I will do is share many ways to help you manage your emotional states so that you can choose happiness *most of the time*. I won't only tell you what you can do, I'll show you *how* to do it. You just have to follow through with the actions.

I'll start right away by sharing my **4 Step Goal-Achieving Formula**. This formula is extremely valuable because you can be doing it without even realizing what you're doing, and it still works!

4 STEPS TO GETTING ANYTHING YOU WANT

Step 1: Know what you want
Step 2: Believe you can have it
Step 3: Plan
Step 4: Take action and remain flexible

Step 1
Know What You Want

When it comes to deciding what you want, it's important that you're as specific and as detailed as possible. It is also imperative that you write what it is that you want down on paper. If it's a car that you want, you want to know the make, the model, and the year, as well as the color of the exterior and interior.

In this first step, there is no such thing as too much detail. Be extremely clear and add attributes as soon as you think of them. Do research on what you want and find out as much as you possibly can about what it is that you want. Feed your senses with detailed images, sounds, and/or experiences when possible.

It is also important to start with smaller goals and work your way up to larger more challenging goals as your confidence grows and your goal-achieving strength increases. If you aim too high on the first try and fail, you may lose steam. Although, I do believe failure can be good for you, a series of small successes—such as completing a crossword puzzle, cooking a dinner that your family loves, or losing a couple of pounds in a week—will build up your self-confidence. Setting a goal of losing 100 pounds in a month might not be a good idea, and it isn't very healthy either.

Step 2
Believe You Can Have It

You have to believe that you can have what you want. It is essential that you choose something that you honestly feel that you can have and for which you have a strong desire. You must expect to achieve your outcome!

If you already had what you wanted, how would it feel? Allow yourself to feel those feelings.

What if you don't believe that you can have that outcome?

Well, there are many techniques that can help you to positively influence your beliefs, and I'll give you the three methods that I currently use on a regular basis. The first is meditation, the second is a visualization technique, and the third is to state positive affirmations.

Meditation: Different forms of meditation have been practiced by all types of people for over 5,000 years. Meditation is a form of contemplation.

When I meditate, I go to the same place in my home each morning (unless of course I'm traveling; in that case I'll find a special place to meditate). I take a few deep breaths, close my eyes, and contemplate being present in this moment in time. I don't focus on the past or the future, I focus on the now. I focus on each breath.

Do other thoughts come into my mind? Of course. That is one reason why it is referred to as a "practice." I'll let the extraneous thoughts flow through, and practice bringing my mind back to the present; back to each breath.

Some people do what is called Mantra Meditation where you focus on a particular word such as "love," or a sound like "Om." I don't place any particular time limit on my process. Sometimes I meditate for just a few minutes and sometimes I meditate for as long as 45 minutes to an hour. I don't have many rules when it comes to meditation, except that I'm 1) sitting quietly, 2) being present, and 3) doing it at least once daily.

There are many books and lots of research on the benefits of meditation and different practices and methods. Meditation makes you "feel" better and you have to remember that feelings are like magnets. Once you are feeling good, good things are attracted to you. Surely, you've had a morning when you woke up feeling on top of the world, and everything went smoothly throughout your day. It was as if the universe was laying gifts at your feet. The opposite happens when you are feeling down. Again, feelings are like magnets.

Personally, meditation has decreased the level of negative stress in my life and has helped me clarify my perspective on many things. Maybe taking the time to relax your mind daily will help you think more clearly as well. My suggestion is to look into several types of meditation and experiment with which one works best for you. Meditation has been an invaluable practice in my life; if you need a calming stress reliever that is always at your fingertips, and won't cost you a dime, I highly recommend that you meditate at least once per day.

Visualization: In this context, visualization is basically a productive form of daydreaming where you imagine that you are experiencing your goals in the present moment.

I highly recommend Shakti Gawain's book, *Creative Visualization*. It is an easy and quick read with many useful examples. I'll share one example using a drop-top red Corvette as our goal.

Find a comfortable place to sit where you feel safe and won't be disturbed. Next, close your eyes and take a few moments to enter a relaxed state. Once you are in a calm and relaxed state, begin to imagine your ideal scene. It is a beautiful, sunny day outside and as you look through the window from inside you see the leaves rustling slightly as the gently-blowing wind moves through them. You think to yourself, "Another perfect day to go for a drive in my new red Corvette."

As you approach your car you start to feel a bit giddy inside and you catch a glimpse of your reflection from the shine on your ride; you are smiling from ear to ear. You click the alarm button to unlock your car and hear the sweet sound of your horn chirp. As you open the door, you smell that wonderful new car aroma. When you sit down, the seat hugs your bottom like a warm welcome home. You start the car and feel the engine purr. Your favorite CD is already in and your departure music comes on. You press the convertible release button, hear it click, and as the top goes back you feel the warm sun on your face. You reach for your glasses and feel them comfortably slide behind your ears. You put the car in drive and love that feeling of excitement rushing back to you.

You are off for a sightseeing drive with no time limit. You turn the corner and you see a friend. She smiles a great big grin at you because she is happy to see you in your new car. The friend then waves hello; you return the smile and wave back at your friend. The wind feels great in your hair as you drive...

As you return home and park your car, you take a moment to admire the details of the interior. Take as much time as you need to fully revel in this experience. Live it now.

After you have taken your time, bring yourself back to where you started. You are now back in your comfortable seat at home, thankful for the experience you just had. You gradually open your eyes and say, "This or something better is now manifesting in my life." Then repeat this statement three times out loud. "I am wide awake, feeling great, and in perfect health!"

This is a great exercise to do directly after you complete your morning meditation and before you do your morning affirmations. I suggest this order for several reasons. I meditate first thing, because my mind is still pretty clear when I first wake up. Then after I meditate, I do my visualizations. I don't have to worry about getting into a relaxed state because I have just finished meditating. Then after the visualization exercise, I do my affirmations.

This order is great for reaffirming your visualizations

and it is also great for those people who have felt like they were being untrue by stating their affirmations in the present tense. The more vivid and real you make your visualizations, the more enthusiastic you can be about your affirmations, because you did in fact just experience what you are affirming.

Productive imagination plus strong feelings with the right actions will attract your goals to you much more quickly. Your feelings are like magnets and as you use these tools to influence your feelings, you are also influencing your circumstances. There are two things that I can not stress enough and they are "Productive Action," and "Living Visualizations." With Living Visualizations you experience the visualization with all of your senses as though you are in that moment right now. You are not only seeing pictures, you are also feeling the feelings, smelling the smells, and hearing the sounds.

Affirmations: What you think about the majority of your day affects your attitude and your actions. When done correctly, affirmations can influence your thoughts productively. They should be stated in the positive present tense as though you already have what you want. It is also necessary that you state your affirmations with emotion.

You may want to start out repeating your affirmations for five to ten minutes, several times a day with your first session in the morning before you start your day. A few examples of affirmations are as follows:

> *I am a superb time manager!*
> *I have excellent listening skills!*
> *I am more and more creative every day!*
> *I feel happy, I feel healthy, I feel terrific!*
> *I am so grateful that I have become a more loving person!*
> And of course:
> *I enjoy driving my drop-top red Corvette!*

Step 3
Plan, Plan, Plan

The next step is to review your plan regularly, revise it when necessary, and refresh or renew your plan as you or your circumstances change. Planning is an ongoing, unavoidable process, so you might as well create a way to look forward to it.

How do you come up with a plan?

There are many ways to devise a plan. One of the ways that I go about creating a plan is by starting with the end goal and working backwards.

For example, when I wanted to complete the audio CD version of this book, the first thing I did was pick up a CD jacket of another self-development program that I had at home and read it word for word. I looked at who was involved in the creation of that product and then I made a list to prioritize later. From looking at the CD, I learned that I needed a graphic designer, a recording and mastering studio, a manufacturer, and an editor as well as other creative people to help with the production. I then searched out other people who had already completed CDs and asked them questions while revising my plan in the process. Did things go wrong in the process? Yes, many things went wrong and my plan had to be revised several times, but in the end, I was able to accomplish my goal using this method.

Another way to create a plan is by using the Internet. The Internet is quite possibly the most useful tool created in modern times. Search engines will lead you to a wealth of information from people who have "been there, and done that." "How to" books, biographies, and competent coaches or mentors (this is one of the best ways to accomplish your goal, and it can save you time and money) will lead you on the right path. Anything that you want to achieve, someone has probably already done it or something similar. You don't have to reinvent the wheel, sometimes you just have to revise it to fit whatever it is that you're using to travel through this journey.

Step 4
Take Action and Be Flexible in Your Approach

It is important to persevere, be tenacious, and take balanced action with flexibility. You're not just taking action so that you can say you did something; you're taking appropriate action to move you closer to your goal. Thomas Carlyle said that "Nothing is more terrible than activity without insight." I'll discuss an interesting example of flexibility in the following section.

The Story of Greyhound

Here is a story about a friend of mine that exemplifies these steps.

My friend always knew what he wanted; he wanted to be an architect. He also believed whole-heartedly that he could do it. He created a plan and he took a lot of productive action. He was accepted into a Masters program in his chosen field at a University located just a few hours away. On the morning before his classes started, he took the Greyhound bus down to his new school. (His actual nickname is Greyhound by the way.) Greyhound was wearing a backpack and carrying a duffle bag with the rest of his belongings. When he arrived at his new school he went directly to the Registrar's office, bags in tow, and paid his fees for the first semester down to the penny.

Then he went to the exact bench on campus where he had made prior arrangements to meet a friend that he was going to live with.

Well, he got to the bench and waited and waited... and waited for the friend. The friend never arrived. Several hours passed and the friend never showed up. He tried to locate the friend to no avail. Now, he didn't know anyone else in the city and since he had used up all of his money for the fees, he didn't have any money left for a hotel.

Now, it was time for some real flexibility. He had to get really creative. He hung out in the building where his classes were supposed to start the next day, and after the building closed for the night, he realized that he had to hide from the janitors. When the janitors finally left, Greyhound was locked inside of the building. He came out of hiding, washed up, used the restroom, scrounged for food, and slept under his drafting board for the next three months. He was basically a prisoner in his classroom.

This actually turned out to be a blessing in disguise, because he couldn't do anything but study and complete his projects. He ended up doing really well in school. So well that he was offered scholarships, found a place to live, and eventually graduated. After graduation, he found a great job and continues to be a successful professional to this day. Greyhound has exceeded his own expectations. To this day, he continues to do very well and owns several homes, several cars, lives a successful, happy, and fulfilling life. He continues to use these principles today. Greyhound's story exemplifies the power of perseverance and flexibility.

The U.S. Constitution doesn't guarantee happiness, only the pursuit of it. You have to catch up with it yourself.

- Benjamin Franklin

6 PRINCIPLES FOR JOY AND FULFILLMENT IN YOUR LIFE S.M.I.L.E.S.

Joy and Fulfillment starts with S.M.I.L.E.S.

S. SELF-LEADERSHIP

M. MASTER CHANGING YOUR PERSPECTIVE

I. INFINITE GRATITUDE

L. LOVE UNCONDITIONALLY

E. EXTRAORDINARY FORGIVENESS

S. SUPERIOR SERVICE

I chose the acronym S.M.I.L.E.S. to describe this point, because smiling alone can make you or someone else feel better. In fact, here is an exercise that you can do right now.

<u>Smile Factor</u>

Wherever you are at this moment, just start smiling. Really, start smiling right now, and smile genuinely. Smile an "I feel good just because" smile. A huge "show all your teeth" smile.

Now, I want you to turn that smile into a huge grin. Now, turn that grin into a laugh; a really good, hearty laugh. Laugh heartily and laugh often. After doing this exercise, absorb the good feelings your body has just produced. It has been proven that laughter creates endorphins in your body that can heal the body and the soul. That's one of the reasons why people love to be around comedians and other funny people who keep them laughing. So, smile and laugh often. It's not only good for you; it also leaves you feeling fulfilled and full of joy. That is where the acronym S.M.I.L.E.S. comes from.

SELF-LEADERSHIP

There are many action steps detailing how to promote self-leadership in the 30 ways in 30 days section of this book (coming later). Self-leadership can be summed up in two words: taking responsibility. Be responsible and you will be a successful "self-leader." It's as simple as that.

Happiness is a choice; it's not something to be put off until you reach all of your goals. Be happy right now!

Happiness is a moment by moment choice. You can have it the moment you decide to choose it. So, choose happiness. Self-leadership is not only about taking responsibility, it is also about having the courage to take appropriate action.

Windows of Opportunity...

Many years ago, I met this wonderful woman through a friend of mine. If you know what it is like to meet someone and become instant friends, you will have a very clear picture of how my relationship with this particular woman was from the start. We would hang out regularly and enjoy a lot of time with each other. As time passed, my feelings for this particular lady started to grow stronger and stronger.

I remember her telling me one day that she'd recently started dating someone and he asked her to marry him. Well, as you can imagine, I was a little shocked because my feelings had started to grow for her. I immediately told her that he wasn't the one for her. I said "From your description of him, it doesn't seem as though he has the proper temperament to be with you. You need someone like me."

I went home that night and couldn't sleep a wink. I thought about how I was going to lose my best friend, who I was in love with. I thought to myself "If I don't take action, I am going to lose her."

The next day, I decided that this was the day that I would make my move. We were driving down the street and stopped at Johnny Rockets on Melrose. I said to her,

"This is the perfect place for our first date." She protested and told me several times that we were just friends. We argued back and forth the entire evening about whether we were in fact on a date or not. As we left the restaurant, the guy behind the counter smiled and said "good luck!" I replied, "Oh we don't need luck; we'll be fine. Thanks anyway."

As we parted ways that night, I gave her a kiss on the cheek as normal and said goodbye. Three days later, we had our first real kiss. A year and half later, we were engaged, and soon after that we were married. We continue to have a loving and productive relationship to this day.

I shared that little story with you because it's one of courage. It's about having the courage to take action. Words cannot express how much that one decision to take action has complemented the happiness I enjoy in my life today.

The man who makes everything that leads to happiness depends upon himself, and not upon other men, has adopted the very best plan for living happily.

- Plato

MASTER CHANGING YOUR PERSPECTIVE

You have the amazing ability to change your perspective instantly. By changing your perspective you can change your emotions and your outlook. You can do this in several ways. One way you can change your perspective is by asking yourself questions. Two questions that I frequently ask myself are:

1. What did I learn from this situation?
2. How can I use what I learned to help myself or someone else in the future?

When I was in college, it was a big deal for me—just to be there. The day of my graduation was a huge celebration; my family and friends were there and it was just wonderful. I remember being so excited as I walked down the aisle to get my diploma.

Of course, when you walk across the stage you don't get the real diploma. I had to go back to the Registrar's office to get the real thing.

I remember the day that I went to get my diploma at the counter. As I waited in line, I was so excited to finally get that degree. The clerk behind the counter was just doing her daily job, and she simply pulled my diploma from a stack of them that were filed in alphabetical order. I had to sign something and then I walked out.

I remember walking away from the counter that day feeling so disappointed. The experience of "getting my actual degree" was so anti-climatic; in fact, it was one of the most anti-climatic experiences in my life. Here I had spent so much time in school and all that I received was this piece of paper. Plus, I didn't even remember too much of what I'd learned over those past few years. So, as I was walking down the street headed towards home, I was definitely despondent.

I started thinking to myself, "What were the last few years about? I've invested all of this time and energy, and I can't even really remember what I learned, except how to do research!" I then used the first question outlined above. Then it dawned on me: I learned how to learn. That was what it was all about.

I realized that by learning how to learn I could obtain any information or knowledge that I desired. Just that one change in perspective helped me see the value of my education and all of the experiences that went with it. Thank you University of Pittsburgh!

"Happy is he who learns to bear what he cannot change."

- J.C.F. Von Schiller

INFINITE GRATITUDE

Being thankful is one of the easiest ways to change your state to a positive one. When you invest time focusing on what you're thankful for, it helps to increase your good feelings.

We will talk about this more later, but I learned an exercise from Oprah. She writes down five things that she is grateful for before she goes to bed. I think that this is a fantastic exercise to do just before sleeping.

I am not one to watch the news at night, because I don't want to go to bed with the negativity that the news reports in my psyche. I prefer to have positive feelings or thoughts on my mind right before drifting into sleep, instead of the sometimes sensational reports that are delivered regularly on local news. So my wife and I came up with another way of doing this exercise. Before going to sleep each night, we share at least five things that we are grateful for from that day. It could be taking a hot shower, having a nice drive to work that morning, or closing a big deal at work. What we have found is that we often have *more* than five things that we're grateful for. Sometimes the list extends to fifteen, twenty, or more.

So before you go to bed tonight, take out a pen and a pad of paper to do this exercise. Just write down five small (or large) things that you are grateful for from your day. You may find that there are more wonderful things going on in your life than you first realized! Think about this: there are some people in this world who don't have running water in their homes. How many times do we take a nice hot shower for granted?

"Happiness lies in the consciousness we have of it."
- George Sand

LOVE UNCONDITIONALLY

You must love unconditionally.

When you can allow yourself to have true, unconditional love in your heart, you may experience a joy that cannot be described with words. The closest word that comes to mind is "bliss."

I personally started to feel this strong feeling when I started to examine my own fears, insecurities, and flaws. Once I started to accept myself and my shortcomings, I stopped judging others as much as I had been. I then started to realize that most people are doing the best that they can with what they have at any given moment in time. You can't give what you don't have, so you first have to learn to love yourself fully and unconditionally before you can unconditionally love others.

"I love myself when I am laughing."
- Zora Neale Hurston

Extraordinary forgiveness

Forgiveness has played one of the most pivotal roles in my own personal happiness. I learned at a very young age that unfortunate things can happen in life. You have to do your best to deal with those challenges, let them go, and move on. I do believe that it is very important to deal with an issue and ultimately important to forgive. By forgiving someone who has wronged you, you are freeing yourself from unnecessary pain and anguish.

You will read more about my childhood later on in this book, but to say that it was an unfortunate one is an understatement. When I was eight years old, I witnessed a man shoot my mother and step-father in cold blood. After working through this tragedy without the help of therapists, and by using some of the principles that I'm sharing with you in this book, united with the love and support of my grandmother, family, and friends, I was able to forgive the man responsible and set myself free.

How was I able to forgive such an atrocity? Well to say I was able to release it and let it go may sound nice, but it would not be the truth. To say that I am a fan of the idea of "forgiving and forgetting" would also be an untruth. I am more of a fan of forgiving and learning from the experience. I have no interest in forgetting what happened; it has helped to shape who I am, and how I want to affect the world. It has given me the desire to positively affect someone else that may be in a similar situation, or in a generally bad place in their life, where they may even want to take their life or the life of another. My purpose, to inspire Greatness in myself and in others, actually may have spawned from the unfortunate events that I experienced.

So, how did I forgive? Well, it started with me asking myself questions. Questions like: Is there any way that I can bring my mother back? Is there any way that I can change what happened? Later on, after realizing that I could not change the situation, I started to ask myself more productive questions like: How can I change my feelings about what happened? How can I be more loving to those around me now? Is there anything good that came from this happening? It took a lot of courage to ask that last question, and even more courage to answer it in the affirmative. It was not easy, but answering that tough question was one of the best things I have ever done.

It does take plenty of courage to forgive. It also takes strength to forgive. And sometimes it takes time to forgive. Something that you must be able to do during this forgiveness process is find something productive to be passionate about. For me it was athletics, for someone else it could be a hobby such as sketching landscapes or playing an instrument. It could be attending Salsa dance classes. Even if you do need to seek out the help of a certified professional, do so. Whatever you need to do productively in order to get to that place of forgiveness, do it and do it now!

Keep in mind that I've been speaking of forgiving someone else when sometimes the person that you need to forgive is yourself. I hope that by sharing my own personal story I will give someone else the courage to set themselves free through forgiveness.

"How unhappy is he who cannot forgive himself."
                                                        - Publilius Syrus

Superior service

All of the principles that I have discussed are very important when choosing happiness. However, if I were asked to sum it all up into just one principle, I would have to say that Service is the master key to happiness.

There are many ways to serve, and one way isn't any more significant or meaningful than another. Preparing a great meal for your family is just as important as an architect building a bridge that transports thousands of people on a daily basis. It's quite interesting to find creative ways to serve.

A Story from the Psychiatric Hospital

I once worked on a 15 patient psychiatric unit as a Milieu Therapist in Pittsburgh, PA. One night, I got a call from the unit where I worked, and they said that they needed me there immediately. The children that I worked with on the unit were apparently not behaving well and were all flipping out simultaneously. The kids were screaming and shouting and running all over the unit in a dangerous manner. They were acting uncharacteristically wild.

I observed the situation, and then I started jumping on the furniture, doing flips, screaming, and pretty much acting in the manner that they were acting. One by one, the kids stopped doing what they were doing and started to stare at me. When all of the kids had halted, I then carried on for another five or ten seconds, and then I stopped. I then told them that they looked exactly like me. They did not like what they saw. They all shook their heads and went back into their rooms and everyone was quiet. It's a funny story, but it was a creative way for me to serve them and the hospital staff.

"One of the things I keep learning is that the secret of being happy is doing things for other people."
- Dick Gregory

RUMINATIONS (My Journey So Far)

WHERE IT ALL STARTED...

While reading this book, you may have been wondering, "What qualifies this guy to tell me how to choose happiness (most of the time)?" Well, anyone who knows me personally will tell you that I have made an art form of it.

What many people *don't* know about me are the many struggles that I went through starting at a very early age.

Now, everyone has their own issues to deal with, and my issues or circumstances are no more or less important than yours. I am simply using my life story as a conduit for expressing the outlined principles and how I used these principles to overcome my own personal struggles.

Why am I telling this story now? Because after so many years, I finally realize that these principles have worked for me on a continual basis, without fail. If applied to your own situation, they may help you to overcome a particular obstacle or to show you a more productive perspective. In my writings, I will share some of my deepest thoughts to give you a true picture of my life and how I used—and continue to use—certain tools to turn a horrifying childhood into a life of adventure and happiness.

Some of these lessons I discovered on my own, while some of them I absorbed from family, friends, teachers, and coaches. I have learned certain other principles from various disciples of personal growth and self-development. The principles are timeless and invaluable, and if used regularly are guaranteed to produce positive results. If only one person is inspired by my story, writing this book was a worthwhile endeavor.

IT COULD HAVE BEEN WORSE

My early childhood was a traumatic one. It was not one that conjures up fond memories of ice cream at the park, vacations at the beach, or a loving, safe household. I was born on March 31, 1969, in Chicago, Illinois to Margaret Jean Burton and Larry (Billy) Burton. I don't remember too much about the very early years, but I do remember when my mother and biological father split up. As you can imagine, any divorce or breakup can be a difficult thing for a child of four or five years old to cope with.

The constant arguing and abuse that my mother endured was difficult for me to watch and understand at that tender, young age. I wasn't really that close to my father, so the fact that he wasn't around after the divorce wasn't the most difficult thing for me to deal with. The hardest thing for me to watch—and not have the power to do anything about—was seeing my mother (a young woman of around twenty-three years old at the time) struggle and learn to cope on her own as a single parent while working a full-time job and going to school at night. She now had two young children (my first sister was born a few years after me) and was constantly struggling to make ends meet. When I look back at pictures during that time, I see the sadness in my eyes and the fear in hers.

We lived in the depths of Chicago, specifically the projects on the south side of Chicago. Picture a depressed area of a highly populated city with unclean streets, overcrowded living and working conditions, graffiti-covered walls, and overpopulated high-rise apartment buildings. Drug dealers and their customers would line the streets like white picket fences did in other, better areas. Instead of the melodic sound of ice-cream vans, the constant ringing of gunshots and glass breaking were a part of normal daily life for me. If there was one word to describe this place, it would be "hell." I often get sad when I think about it because it is still a reality for so many families today who are living below the poverty line in the ghettos of our cities and towns. Talk of drugs, death, and crime were the subject matter of daily conversations amongst the young and the old.

I know that my mother feared for her life and ours on a daily basis. I remember the period of time in our lives when she would carry a gun in her pocket with her finger poised on the trigger as we walked through the neighborhood back to our apartment. I'm sure she probably wondered how we would be affected by our surroundings as adults since she was going to school to try and provide us with a better life. She wanted us to have a reality better than this.

It was hard to shield a curious male child from all that was going on. She tried to do so as much as she could. There was no male figure in the household, so I often felt like I needed to take on that role. I was a serious, contemplative young boy, and very protective of my sister and my mother. I remember spending a lot of time alone. I didn't complain when we went to bed hungry and cold, I didn't complain for not having the toys that I wanted, nor did I speak up when both physical and mental abuse of the most horrific kind was inflicted upon me by the other boys in the neighborhood for not hanging out at all hours of the night. I often cried at night as I watched my mother sleep, wondering if she would ever be happy and live the life that she truly deserved. In my own way, I prayed for her happiness and ours.

A few years after the divorce, my mother met an older man: Arthur Day. He went by the name "Arte." Arte was a tall man whose look was intimidating. His skin was the color of charcoal and his voice was deep, authoritative, and strong. He was a community leader and a martial arts expert. When I first met him, I was fascinated by his chiseled physique and excited at the prospect of becoming tall and strong like he was through this unfamiliar practice of martial arts. Soon after Arte and my mother met, she fell in love with him (or the idea of him) and they were married. I now had a step-father.

For a fleeting moment, I felt as though my prayers had been answered and my dreams were about to come true. In the early days, I would see my mother smiling more, carrying herself differently, and having the look of hope in her eyes. We quickly moved from our place into his small apartment in the projects. It was now the five of us (he had a daughter from a previous relationship) sharing a small space in an area that was far worse than where we lived before.

It was soon after we moved in that the abuse began. Although I am a tall, muscular 6'4" man now, back then I was small for my age and had a slight frame for a six-year-old. After a few drinks in the evening (vodka was his drink of choice), I became a punching bag for this man who was four times my size. Blood was drawn regularly and my small six-year-old frame was continually bruised and broken from the almost daily torture. Sometimes the abuse wasn't physical; it was mental. The unnecessary taunting during the day would haunt me at night. Other times, it was simple food deprivation as a form of punishment. My crime: being an inconvenient male child.

Because my mother was striving for a better life, I believe she intentionally turned a blind eye to the abuse. I would often see her with bruised limbs too, and knew that she too was dealing with the abuse that he was inflicting upon her. It was soon apparent that we were in a worse off position than before, and I saw my mother's dejected spirit return more aggressively. After some time, I became numb to the pain—both emotionally and phys- ically. This was my new way of life, and shutting down was my way of coping with it.

My step-father managed a recreation center in one of the parks in another neighborhood, and my mother would also take on extra work shifts to help the family out. During this time, she fell pregnant with another baby girl, and our family of five swelled to six. This was yet another mouth to feed, and another life that they were responsible for. As an adult now, I can't even fathom the pressure that they were under. My mother was still going to school, still working a full-time job, and still looking after the kids.

The recreation center became a kind of haven of sorts for me. When we would go there while my parents were working, I was permitted to roam the grounds, explore, and play freely. When allowed to do this, it was a freeing, fleeting moment of normality for me. I could escape the nightmare of my home life on the playground, and be somewhere and someone else for a few hours. I cherished my time spent there. I filled those hours with as much as possible so that I could savor those memories at home when my reality set in. I was just eight years old when my life and my reality took another drastic turn.

My life changed one sunny but windy Chicago day in October of 1977. It was a very nice day for that time of year, but just a regular day like any other in my eight-year-old existence. My younger sisters were 7, 6, and 13 months old respectively. It was one of the days that we got to go to the recreation center and I would get to escape for a few golden hours. My sisters were playing loudly together; laughing and having fun. I was in my own world on one of the semi-functioning toys on the playground. It didn't matter that I was alone playing; all that mattered was that I was free. In my world, when I was playing and closed my eyes, dreams of fast cars, planes, and speed would occupy my mind. I can't remember where my mind was that day, probably flying down a freeway in a sports car. We had been at the park for an hour or so, and I was in heaven. What followed then was one of the most horrifying and surreal moments of my life. I definitely understand when people talk about how some of life's moments occur in slow motion. I heard a strange popping sound in the distance, but paid it no mind. As I slid down the slide, just like I would have on any other ordinary day, I looked around and saw a huge, angry looking man taking huge steps towards me. The look in his eyes was one of wrath. Even during the times of enduring the abuse from my step-father and from the boys around the way, I'd never seen this look in anyone's eyes before. He was about 6 foot tall, which to me as a child was huge. He looked somewhat disheveled and mentally disturbed or tormented in some way.

I stood frozen for what seemed like hours, not knowing what to do or say. At about fifteen feet away, he made direct eye contact with me, but he said and did nothing. I knew that something was terribly wrong. At that point my eyes gazed from the furious look in his eyes down his tattered torso to see what he was carrying, firmly and strongly with both hands. I'd only seen a gun like the one he was carrying in movies; the piece of machinery looked bigger than me. It was a very long, larger than life automatic rifle. It then dawned on me that the *"Pop, Pop, Pop"* that I had heard just seconds before were in fact shots from his gun. As my eyes slowly made their way back back up to his face, our eyes locked again, but he did and said nothing. Then he charged forward.

As he brushed past me, the gunman took large purposeful strides and headed straight over to my step-father Arte. Arte at the time was on a ladder repairing one of the swing sets. As he turned and saw the gunman, I could see the recognition in Arte's eyes. He jumped down in one motion and lifted the ladder with both hands to charge the crazed man in an attempt to defend himself. The gunman clearly had the upper hand as he stood in front of Arte and shot him three times, squarely in the chest. The sound of the shots reverberated throughout my entire body. With each ring my small chest exploded again and again with fright. My step-father wasn't a weak man, but he collapsed like a ton of bricks right there in front of me. I watched intensely as the blood began to pour from his chest profusely and his eyes rolled to the back of his head in defeat. I didn't see him move at all and I knew that he was dead upon impact. The blood continued to pour and formed a large irregular circle around him, soaking his shirt, arms, and hands. I locked eyes with the gunman for one last time before he calmly walked away from the scene. I ran to look for my mother and soon learned that the *Pop, Pop, Pop* sound that I had heard earlier were shots that were aimed at her. She lay yards away in her own pool of blood from the three shots that had penetrated her abdominal area, yet she was still alive. In a matter of minutes, my eight-year-old mind had to grasp a horrifying reality and assume the biggest responsibility of my life.

I ran to gather my sisters, who were obviously at the

time hysterical, and instructed them to remain calm. We all hid in a group for a few moments for fear that the gunman may return, and then ran to get help. As we turned away from the scene, I remember wanting to feel some pain for my step-father. There he was lying in his own blood, dead, with three large holes in his chest. But I didn't feel any pain for him. I suppose deep down I knew and rationalized that at that moment my nightmare of being abused by him was now over. My mother on the other hand needed help immediately; she was still alive and moving slightly.

Moments later, pandemonium broke out. In what seemed like seconds, there were fire trucks, ambulances, and police cars surrounding the recreation center. There was a flurry of activity when the loud sirens and flashing lights engulfed the area.

My step-father Arte was pronounced dead at the scene. My mother, however, was still alive. My sisters and I were standing with one of the police officers as we watched her being lifted from the ground onto a stretcher by the paramedics. Her body was motionless and her eyes were half-closed. From the corner of my eye, I saw her large, brown, leather purse lying a few feet away from where she had been laying. I wriggled loose, ran over to it quickly, and grabbed it off of the ground. Then I ran over to the moving stretcher and placed it beside her.

"Mom, your purse, don't forget your purse!!" I shouted.

All I can remember after that was the quick slam of the ambulance doors closing and the sound of the blaring siren as it drove away at high speed. Those were the last words I spoke to my mom. She passed away a few short days later.

Couple shot in park; grudge led to twin killing

Oct. 23 19 77

By LAWRENCE MUHAMMAD

While police have discovered no motive for the killing Saturday of 37-year-old Arthur Day and his wife Margurite Burton, neighborhood residents believe the incident may be linked to the arrest of the gunman, Virgil Butler, last July in the shooting of his common-law-wife.

Butler, a 43-year-old security guard, is facing two counts of murder after he allegedly shot the couple at the Bensley Field House at 9700 S. Yates where Day works as a recreation counselor.

Day, who lives at 1440 W. 14th, was pronounced dead on arrival at South Chicago Hospital, and Ms. ████ died early Monday after remaining in critical condition since the shooting. BURTON DAY

Police say that Day, a recreation worker for the Chicago Park District, was tutoring students on the park grounds when Butler arrived and the two began to argue.

According to reports, Butler left angered, returned with a carbine, walked up to Day and fired. Police also said Butler fired three other shots into Day as he lay on the ground. Ms. Burton attempted to flee from the gunman through the field house, but she was shot three times by the gunman.

Although police have termed the incidnet senseless and lacking motive, local residents say the shooting may be the result of a grudge between the two men involving Butler's shooting of his common-law-wife last July.

"He definitely knew the man (Butler)," said Mrs. Juanita Day, mother of the dead man. "Arthur was telling us about it, about how this man shot his wife and how terrible it was."

Mrs. Day charged that Butler shot his wife near the Bensley Fieldhouse where her son heard shots, sheltered the woman from her husband and called police.

Butler's wife later dropped charges against him, but residents familiar with the incident say that Butler may have held a grudge.

"It may sound like conjecture," said Mrs. Dorothy Edwards, a community relations counselor and a friend of the Day couple, "but without this motive the shooting is senseless."

Arthur Day was a graduate student at Northwestern University, and Margurite Burton was a pre-law student at Chicago State University. The couple had four children, 8-year-old LeCrecia, Day's daughter from a previous union, Chappale, 8, Ms. Burton's son from an earlier marriage, 5-year-old Chirette and 13-month-old Abika.

Actual clipping from the event.

40

WHY I SHARE....

I tell you this story of my early childhood because I want to share with you what I went through at a young age as compared to where I am now. You now have an idea of what I have had to overcome in order to get to this place where I choose happiness most of the time. I now see myself as a productive, well-adjusted, happy person...most of the time.

After this traumatic time in my life, I of course had to deal with the regular bumps and bruises that one experiences throughout their teenage years moving forward, but all of those experiences have shaped who I am today. I often used to think that I could have used the events of my childhood as an excuse to become irresponsible, turn to a life of crime, or not do anything at all with my life. Alternatively, I decided that I could use the same events to grow and become an example of what a human being could accomplish in spite of adversity.

We all have our challenges. I don't want others to believe that I think my challenges are worse than theirs. There are many people that have suffered and will suffer far greater than I have. My goal is simply to use my life as an example to give anyone the tools they require to overcome a difficult situation, or to simply live a better, more abundant life. These tools have helped me, and in turn my goal is to help others.

I have had several negative external forces in my life. On the other hand, I have had many positive external forces as well. Both forces have played a part in who I am today, and for that I am grateful. I am grateful for both the good and the bad.

GRANDMOTHER TO THE RESCUE...

After my mother and step-father were killed, my maternal grandmother came to the rescue and saved our lives in more ways than one. My grandmother had nine children of her own, and my mother was one of her oldest. At the time, my grandmother was living in Jamestown, New York. Of course the moment she heard about the murder of her daughter she came to Chicago to get me and my sisters. I will be forever grateful to her for that. There wasn't even a chance for us to be registered and placed into the "system" for foster care. She didn't miss a beat.

My grandmother put us in a totally different environment compared to the one to which we had become accustomed. We went from an overly abusive situation to a loving, nurturing home. We went from barely eating a good meal to an abundance of good food that tasted good simply because it was made with love. We moved from the crowded, violent, hardcore projects on the south side of Chicago to a whole house with a garden in the backyard on a block with trees and beautiful front yards in Jamestown,

New York.

Several interesting things happened shortly there-after. As a child in Chicago with my parents, I suffered from asthma and acute bronchitis. In the projects I suf-fered from severe coughing bouts and frequent painful asthma attacks that would leave me gasping for breath at any random moment. Within a few years of moving in with my grandmother to what I would call an "open-air environment," the asthma and bronchitis disappeared completely. Now I realize how people are able to heal themselves from illnesses. Some people heal themselves by changing their attitudes and environments, and by removing stressful situations from the equation. There is certainly something to be said about peaceful retreats. My grandmother's home for me was that peaceful retreat. For the first time in my life, though it was an eventual process, I stopped living in fear.

The second benefit was a major change in perspective. Over the years that followed, I had frequent recurring nightmares from re-living that day in the park with my mother and step-father. I would often wake up suddenly in the middle of the night screaming for help with my sheets soaking wet from the sweat. I was frequently found sleep-walking, only to be awakened by my grandmother who would then lovingly take me back to bed and stay with me until I fell asleep. For a few years after the incident, I still thought I was living in a nightmare. Then one day, it happened—I literally "woke up" from it all.

AWAKENING

Questions are one of the most powerful tools that we have in this world. When you ask questions, you open yourself up to a world of possibilities, solutions, and insights. I used questions to help me solve my torment and the anger in my life up until that point.

I distinctly remember the day that my questions started to help me. I was walking down 10th Street in Jamestown, and I remember having some distinct thoughts about all of the incidents that had lead to me walking down that street, on that day.

I thought to myself, "Chappale, this is your life. Is this really a nightmare? Is your mother going to come back? Is there anyway that you can change what happened? How can you go forward and live a productive life despite all that you have endured?" I first looked inwards, and then around for the answers. I answered myself by saying, "This is your life, this isn't a nightmare, she isn't ever coming back, and therefore you must live." It was in that very lucid moment that I made a choice to live.

I could have chosen to blame the world. I could have continued to ask myself, "Why? Why me? Why my mother?" but those questions were not going to move me forward. I know that I could have turned to a life of irresponsibility and that the anger that I had inside at the time could have been used in a much different way. People could have justified my negative behavior by saying, "Yes, he had such a rough childhood, you can understand why this happened."

My other choice was to live my life to the best of my ability and be a positive example of what someone can accomplish despite experiencing a great deal of adversity at such a young age.

I clearly remember thinking about which choice I was going to make. One thing that I realized at this very young age was that everything, yes <u>everything</u>, happens for a reason, and that everything happens just the way it is supposed to happen. As hard as that may be to digest, it is my sincere belief that it is true.

Many times, we can't see or understand the things that happen to us, but there is a reason for everything, and that is why we need to be thankful for both the good *and* the bad. I realized this truth and started acknowledging it at a very young age. That doesn't mean that I don't still get upset, hurt, and angry, or that I don't cry when I'm in emotional or physical pain. It doesn't mean that I don't have challenges. However, I do now understand that it is all just a part of this journey we call life, and that those difficult, challenging, and adverse times are events that help us grow as human and spiritual beings.

I am thankful for the time that I had with my mother here on earth, and I can now look back at that series of events and surmise that they happened because they were *supposed* to happen. It could have happened for a variety of reasons; maybe they happened because this book was supposed to be birthed years later to help someone in their journey to fulfill their purpose. Or could it be that this event happened so that I could be the person that I have become today, as opposed to a product of that terrible environment?

It's important for me to say that the purpose of this book is not to be a guide on how to be happy all of the time. I believe emotions are natural, and an important part of life (although there are some people who seem to be peaceful all of the time, for example, Buddhist monks). In my opinion, for us to be in a constant state of happiness is unrealistic and not the goal of this text. I think happiness and sadness are two sides of the same coin. Without one, can you truly have the other?

My point here, and the reason why I titled this book *How to Choose Happiness… Most of the Time*, is because I enjoy the emotions of happiness rather than the emotions of sadness, frustration, or anger. But I do believe that those negative emotions have a place in our life. Sometimes they are necessary to motivate us, and sometimes they are meant to protect us or to simply move us forward in some way.

Some people may say that there is no need to have these negative emotions. I have not yet evolved to the place where I don't see the need for other emotions. So, if you see me on the street one day and I'm not the happy-go-lucky guy that I am *MOST OF THE TIME*, you'll know that this isn't an act; it's a choice. I have an acute awareness that there are times when I am upset, angry, or disappointed. To me, having that variety of emotions makes me a fuller and more complete human being. It helps me appreciate the happiness I feel... when I choose it.

A NEW LIFE.....

Jamestown is a town that will always hold a place in my heart. It was everything that a child my age could ever want. In Jamestown, New York, I had a new lease on life.

I started to become a much more active person. I would start my day with questions like: "How am I going to live fully today?" or "How am I going to have a great day?" I went from a place where there was little or no physical activity, to an environment where I could participate in sports and other activities regularly. I didn't just do one sport, I was on every track team, baseball team, and wrestling team. If there was any other type of sport that I could be a part of, I joined it. I went from little to no activity outside of martial arts, to a schedule packed with practices. In my later years, I became extremely athletic.

There was also something that I sought out in my athletic participation that my grandmother wasn't able to give me: positive male role models. These positive male role models gave me a different sort of nurturing. My biological father is still alive, but we never had that kind of nurturing, father-son relationship, and at that time in my life he was thousands of miles away back in Chicago. (It is important for me to say that I don't hold any negative feelings towards my biological father; he did the best he could with what he had.) Through athletics I found several positive male role models, so I chose to get what I wanted and needed in that respect from that particular place.

There were several coaches (who happened to be men) who helped me steer my life in a certain, positive direction. My grandmother was able to steer my life positively in another way. She gave me as much as she could in terms of love, affection, and care on a day-to-day basis. She instilled certain values and morals in me, and taught me how to be a good person. She was wonderful and I always give her credit as one of the main "molders" of my life. One of the first things that she told us when we got to Jamestown was that we could do anything that we put our minds to. It's funny, because she was the first motivational speaker that I was aware of, and I didn't even think of it that way until I started to write this book.

I can fondly recall the days and evenings that my grandmother would sit down and tell us stories; really interesting stories about her childhood and all of the struggles that she went through. I distinctly remember one story in particular that she used to tell us. It was one of her crowning glories and made her really proud.

My grandmother used to pick cotton; her father was a sharecropper. She would always tell us how much cotton she would pick, and the huge cotton bags that she would fill. She could pick it fast and pick it well. One day her father paired her up with another person's daughter from a neighboring farm. They then had a race and picked cotton from sun up to sun down to see who could pick the most. My grandmother set a goal for herself and said that she picked a few hundred pounds of cotton that day. Now that seems like a lot of cotton! I remember hearing these stories and being inspired by them. She inspired me to set goals and achieve them.

I've never been to a cotton farm and probably will never go to one. I don't even know what a cotton plant looks like, but that story always resonated with me when it came to being the best that I could be in my chosen field or focusing on whatever I put my mind to. Other stories of how she left home at the age of 16 and went from picking cotton to cleaning houses also inspired me. I heard tales of how she adapted to change in many situations. She lived life on her own terms. That is success to me. My grandmother's stories and spirit left me yearning to live a passion-filled life.

A Family Role Model Is Drive To Success

By RANDALL J. SWEENEY

From our early childhood to our later days of life, we are influenced by a number of different people. Our first contacts are primarily family, but that sphere of influence grows as we get older. We find our group of friends and ultimately the wide base of acquaintances to be most influential. The family members — father, mother, brothers and sisters — provide the most influence on what we are and can be. What if mother and father were not there? Who would pick up that role?

In 1977, a young mother dies, leaving behind three small children. Rather than leave these children to be placed in a strange home, her mother steps forward and takes them into her home. This mother, their grandmother, already had eight children but willingly accepted the responsibility of these children — Chappale, 8; Chivette, 6; and Abika Burton, 1. These three children were all very normal. They were full of energy and excitement in all they did. As the years passed, their grandmother provided the direction and helped mold their lives. She kept them focused on getting an education and making the most of their lives. As children, they enjoyed sports, especially running and basketball.

Chappale and Chivette both joined Striders. From the Strider program, they learned many lessons from the competition and their study programs. They were an encouragement to each other and helped keep the focus on success. Behind all of this, their grandmother was the mainstay of their lives. She was always there for that piece of advice and assistance.

In 1986, the Chautauqua Region Community Foundation helped Chappale with a scholarship. He was the recipient of the Maude Grant Kent scholarship. He was accepted at the University of Pittsburgh where he was enrolled in a pre-med curriculum. While at the University of Pittsburgh, he excelled in track and ultimately achieved world distinction. He was a great leader with a positive attitude. His sister, Chivette, received a scholarship at Eastern Michigan University because of their talents in basketball. Abika graduated from high school in the mid-90s and was looking at colleges in Colorado at our last contact.

Article about my grandmother, sisters, and I continued on next page...

50

While at the University of Pittsburgh, Chappale became involved in acting and found his true love. He continued his studies and accepted a job as a milieu therapist in Western Psychiatric Institute and Clinic. At the clinic, he worked with mentally disabled children and received two commendations. Chappale realized that he had a strong desire for the theater. He refocused his career around his acting and spent a great deal of his efforts around teaching acting. He had an ongoing thirst for knowledge and continued his studies in many areas. During that time, he made motivational speeches to many different groups. Chappale has continued his acting. Our last contact indicated that he was in New York City in a drama group off Broadway. He is continuing to take acting lessons and is working some with a movie company. He still is pursuing his true love and what he really enjoys doing.

Chivette completed her studies at Eastern Michigan University and is living in Tennessee.

The success of these young people is a tribute to their grandmother — a person who unselfishly provided them the leadership and the nurturing they very much needed. Both Chappale and Chivette felt that the greatest influence on their lives came from their grandmother, a strong person who was always there for them. Mrs. Davis must be very proud of her grandchildrens' accomplishments.

The Community Foundation is delighted to have played a small role in Chappale's life with a scholarship. It is satisfying to read that the foundation scholarship recipients are achieving good things. If you are interested in starting your own scholarship fund or contributing to an existing fund, this can be accomplished very easily. A scholarship from the Community Foundation will help open many new doors for the recipients.

The Chautauqua Region Community Foundation is located at 21 E. Third St., Suite 301, Jamestown, N.Y.

A WORLD BEYOND JAMESTOWN...

Athletics in high school led me to a world beyond Jamestown. It gave me a different motivation, because not only was I able to see and experience the fullness and serenity of the country, I was also exposed to bigger dreams and other lessons such as discipline (which I needed to stay on the teams I played for), teamwork, leadership, and problem-solving. I also learned the value of recognition. It was a great experience to be able to go to an awards banquet and see others receive a trophy. It was something to aspire to.

I remember when I first joined the track team and one of my classmates, Audra Avery, told me that when you join the team and keep going to practice you get a trophy and a t-shirt.

I had never been exposed to banquets before, nor had I ever won anything. It was such a big deal for me to get my first four inch trophy. It was a whole new world for me which I relished in. I recall a write-up they did on me in the local newspaper and the question was, "How did your track career begin?" My short but sweet answer was that, "it began with a trophy and a t-shirt."

It Started With A T-Shirt

A small trophy and a T-shirt. That's all it took to launch Chappale Burton's track career, which is literally and figuratively growing by leaps and bounds.

"This girl told me, 'Why don't you come out, come to practice," Burton said. "You can get a trophy and a T-shirt."

So Burton, then a sixth-grader, went to the YMCA where the Chautauqua Striders, a youth development program that was just starting to take shape, was holding track practice.

"I never had a trophy," Burton said. "I got my first trophy from the Striders."

Now 18, Burton is setting his sights on this weekend's National Junior Track and Field Championships at the University of Arizona.

A first or second place finish in the 400-meter intermediate hurdles will earn Burton a berth on the National Junior Team, which will tour Havana, Vancouver and Pullman, Wash., in two weeks.

Can he do it?

"It looks hard, but I'm just going for the gusto," Burton said. "I feel like I have a chance if I go out and do my best."

The trials and semifinals will be held Friday. The finals are set for Saturday.

Burton, who just completed his freshman year at the University of Pittsburgh, qualified for the Junior Nationals by running a 53.9 in the 400-meter intermediate hurdles at the Pitt Invitational last month.

Two weeks later, Burton was a member of Pitt's mile relay team that ran a 3:09.4 at the Easterns at Villanova University. That time was the third-fastest in Pitt's history.

CHAPPALE BURTON

Article about how I got involved with track continued on next page...

For his part, Burton ran a quarter-mile split time of 47.65, his personal best at that distance.

— — —

Chalk one up for perseverance.

"His progress is interesting," said Ron Graham, executive director of the Striders. "As a sophomore in high school, his best quarter-mile (time) was 60 (seconds) flat.

— — —

"I talked to "Chop" about his career and about weight training. As a junior, he came down to 52.8 seconds (at the 1985 Junior Olympic Nationals in Seattle). At that point, I realized he had the potential to run the 400 meters."

The following year, his senior year at Jamestown High School, Burton failed to qualify for the state meet, but rebounded to win a bronze medal in the 4x400 relay at the Empire State Games and place fifth in the 400 meters at the Junior Olympic Nationals at Chicago.

— — —

"It was a combination of hard work, determination, weight training and God-given ability," Graham said of Burton's dramatic improvement in two years.

The lanky teen impressed the Pitt coaches enough to put him on the traveling team on both the indoor and outdoor teams this year.

— — —

He was named All-East indoors, running the quarter-mile leg of the distance medley relay and finishing 10th in the 500 meters at the Big East Championships in Syracuse.

Outdoors, Burton made it to the finals in the 400-meter intermediate hurdles at the Big East Championships, where he finished eighth.

— — —

A week after that, Burton qualified for the junior nationals.

"What he did this year is the equivalent of a freshman going in and starting on the football or basketball teams," Graham said.

— — —

And with any luck, Burton will be in the "starting lineup" when the Junior National Team hits the road next week.

Along your journey, you meet some truly special people. Ron Graham was one of those people. He was a strong influence in my life and a lot of other kids' lives. He was the one that started my career in athletics. I have been able to duplicate that "feeling" of goal setting, accomplishment, discipline, teamwork, and problem-solving in many other areas of my life, and I continue to strive towards it.

To this day I am still very active in sports in one form or another, whether it be martial arts, yoga, running, or circuit training. We as human beings are goal-seeking mechanisms. As long as we have something to strive for it helps us with our ultimate goal of happiness. It's not always going to be achieved through athletics, sales, or business for everyone.

There are people who are creative, and they get that same feeling of accomplishment from creating something beautiful like a painting, a sculpture, or a floral arrangement. There are some people who don't compete with other people, but they compete with themselves and get that same "feeling" from going out and running three miles in a designated amount of time by themselves, or by setting a goal of running three miles every day. That is how they achieve that "feeling" of accomplishment.

At this point in my life, I now have that feeling of accomplishment every day. Every single day, I get up at around four AM and practice yoga and meditation. Now that's a huge accomplishment for me. I've accomplished something every day before anything else has even happened, and I really look forward to it. I enjoy being able to say "I practice yoga." Not only do I practice yoga, I can say, "I get up every morning at four in the morning to practice yoga and meditate!" I say that like I have bragging rights or something, but what is really important here is how it makes me feel. My mind, body, and soul seem to be in a better place because of this. The reason I

tell people this is because I know what yoga and meditation has done for me over the years. Also, for me it is like
having a daily anchor. It gives me a bit of stability, and it
is something that I can count on and look forward to. I
don't need any special equipment and I do it wherever I
am in the world.

FORWARD TO COLLEGE...

My track experience started in the 6th grade. I ran
from the 6th grade all the way through high school.
Another major turning point of my life was when my
coach at the time, Ron Graham, asked me what I was
planning on doing after high school. At that point in time
I had made up my mind that I was going to go into the
armed services. I had an uncle who went into the service,
and I remembered his general disposition and demeanor
when he went in. He was out of shape and always looked
a bit scruffy. He went away to the army and when he
came out, after training, he had really changed. He stood
up straight now, had big strong arms (much like those of
my step-father), and was clean-shaven. He looked really
sharp and I wanted to emulate exactly that. He had also
traveled around the world, and there was certainly something to be said for that. He spoke differently, and told me
of different cultures he had experienced and the people

that he had met along the way. Naturally, when everyone was preparing to leave to go to college, I knew that I was leaving, but I didn't think that college was an option. So, in the 10th grade, when Coach Graham asked me that question "What are you going to do after high school?" I told him that I was going into the armed services and that I was going to make a career out of it. I told him why, that my choice was based on what I saw had happened to people who went away to the army. When they came back, they were different. They looked, acted, and sounded different. However, the people who graduated from high school and stayed in the same town didn't seem to exemplify that growth. A lot of them would end up on a certain corner, and year after year they would be in that same place. The change, or what I describe now as the "growth," that I saw was something that appealed to me. They had experienced things, and that was something that was attractive and intriguing to me. I thought that the best way for me to get that was by joining the military.

My coach, perhaps knowing that I didn't think that college was an option, then said, "If you could go to any college, which college would you go to?" I told him right there and then that I'd never even thought about it before. He said, "Well think about it now! If you could go to any college in the whole country, which one would it be?" I said, "OK.... I would want to go to the University of Pittsburgh." At that precise moment he said, "Well, that's where you are going." I said "okay," and it was as simple as that.

It went back to my grandmother telling me, "You can do anything that you put your mind to," but now my mind was made up for me that I was going to the University of Pittsburgh.

I wanted to go to that school because in my travels on the track team, I'd met this gentleman by the name of Roger Kingdom, who ended up becoming a two-time Olympic gold medalist. He won the National 1st place title for the High Hurdles at the NCAA's the year I met him; I was a spectator at that meet. The NCAA's were held at the Carrier Dome in Syracuse, New York. The day that I met Roger, he sat down with me and spent several hours talking with me about setting and achieving goals in life. We were sitting on seats outside of an elevator in the hotel at which we were staying. All of the other college students were partying and having a good time, yet Roger took a few hours out of his evening to talk to me. Those two or so hours had a major influence on my life. Roger was at University of Pittsburgh, so when my coach asked me where I wanted to go, he played a huge part in my answer.

Thereafter, I prepared for the SATs and met another influential person in my life: Nancy Carlson. Mrs. Carlson was the educator that helped me prepare for the SATs and changed my courses around to get me prepared for college. She was the person who drove me down to visit the university. She became another mother figure in my life, and she is probably the person who will be most proud of me for completing this book.

Of the five colleges I applied to, I got into the University of Pittsburgh. Of course the first thing that I wanted to do at Pitt was to run track. The ironic thing was that I went there because of Roger Kingdom, and when I got there Roger had actually finished his time as a member of the track team. Even though he wasn't running for the school anymore, he would still practice with the team sometimes, and when I finally met him again, he actually remembered me. That was a great feeling! Roger is really a wonderful person and bumping into him again really confirmed that I had come to the right place. We practiced together a few times which was an amazing experience for me. Another one of my dreams had come true. He was a two-time gold medalist, and not only did he take the time out to speak with me about going to college, but here I was at college and he was taking the time out to practice with me. I appreciated his genuine nature very much. He is one of the most down-to-earth people I know.

To this day, I like to take the time out to speak with kids and younger people; you never know the effect that you will have on someone else's life. When I was on my way to college, some of my friends were getting scholarships. I was *just* starting to do really well in high school so I didn't have a scholarship at that time. The University of Pittsburgh was a Division 1 school, and there was only one other school at the time that was showing some interest in having me run track for them. I obviously had already made up my mind and only wanted to go to the University of Pittsburgh.

At the University of Pittsburgh, I "walked" onto the track team. Being a "walk on" means that you don't have a scholarship; you are basically trying out for the team. I walked onto the team and immediately learned the meaning of the word "perseverance."

The experience I had on the track team also helped me to increase my level of discipline. I now had to compete with others who had earned scholarships and who were some of the best in the country. Healthy competition in my mind had always been good. I drew on stories from my grandmother about being the best that you can be at whatever you decide to do. Well, in order for me to gain a spot on the track team, I had to step it up more than a few notches. I then chose to really put my mind to it and devise a program. This all goes back to planning and taking flexible action. I chose to get up at four every morning and run up and down hills wearing heavy combat boots (you now see where the four AM habit came from). I would do that for one hour every day and then get cleaned up for classes. In the afternoon I would attend track practice, and then I would go to my room and rest or hang out with friends. This was my regime during my freshman year.

That year was the first time in my life that I had been away from home, and it was extremely overwhelming in many ways. It was a wonderful experience, but also when you get a bit of freedom, that old adage can ring true: give a person enough rope and they can hang themselves or pull themselves up with it. Well, in my freshman year there was a lot of freedom. I enjoyed that freedom so much that I almost failed out of school because my focus on my studies had waned. My main focus was track and friends. I was put on academic probation, which meant that if I didn't raise my grades to a 2.5 GPA by the end of the following semester I would have to sit out for a full year. So at the end of my freshman year I was on academic probation coming back to the beginning of the year.

I rationalized that I had an opportunity, and if I missed this window I would end up going back home to Jamestown, the place that I wanted to leave so that I could grow and see the world through a different set of eyes. I had an opportunity to go to college and when it came to my studies I wasn't really applying myself enough, so much so that I was about to allow myself to fail out. One day I took some time out to think. I just spent the day thinking about the reason why I had chosen to go to college and what my ultimate goal was. I then made a choice that failing out of school simply was not going to happen to me.

I started reviewing my goals each and every day, and examining why was I there. Every morning I was reminded of the reason **why** I came to college. This helped me stay focused and on course. When I came back to school my sophomore year, not only did I maintain the ability to stay in school, but I also earned a scholarship, which was an amazing accomplishment. Just that slight change in perspective, how I was looking at things, turned my course around and set me in the right direction. Thereafter, I had an excellent and productive track *and* academic career. I raised my GPA up to a point where I could stay in school, and I even made the Dean's List for one or two semesters thereafter. I volunteered at one of the local hospitals, joined a fraternity, which changed my life, and I was also the homecoming king for the University of Pittsburgh.

One of my most important major accomplishments was being part of a record-breaking mile relay team in track. By my senior year at Pitt, I was the team captain and the most valuable player (MVP). Out of all of the trophies and plaques that I have ever received in my life that is the one that I have always kept. I still look at that trophy as a sign of accomplishment and motivation to this day. It all goes back to what my grandmother would say "You can do whatever you put your mind to." College was an amazing experience, and of course I graduated with a degree in psychology.

SELF-DEVELOPMENT...

During all of the experiences I endured as a child, I never received any therapy. The only therapy that I had was self-imposed. I spent a lot of time alone thinking, and I also spent a lot of time talking with friends. I have often said that if everyone had one good friend that could listen to them, there would be a decreased need for psychotherapists, because that is essentially what the good psychotherapists do: listen and help you productively reflect. I don't want to simplify the profession, but that is really what they do; they are very good "professional listeners." I do believe that they should be paid very well for it, because listening is a skill that many have challenges mastering. I gravitated towards the psychology field in college because it was interesting to me. I enjoyed the study of the mind, how it works, and how and why people do what they do. I didn't realize at the time that I was drawn towards that field of study because I basically still needed to work through some of my issues. As I stated earlier, I have never had any therapy to deal with my trauma, but I've done a lot of soul-searching and self-therapy. Through reading, reflecting, participating in stress relieving athletics, and meditation I have been able to heal myself. I always say that "Meditation is my medication." To clear your mind on a daily basis is one of the biggest gifts that you can give to yourself.

THE TRUTH ABOUT THERAPY...

Because of my interest in psychology, I thought that I would eventually go to medical school and become a psychiatrist. At the time, my purpose for wanting to do that was to help people. I reasoned that I wanted to help people; I wanted to talk with people about their problems and issues in order to help them work through these issues in the same way that I had been able to.

Soon after college, I had the opportunity to work at one of the leading psychiatric hospitals in Pittsburgh for several years as a milieu therapist. I met some really wonderful and dedicated people there. They loved their jobs and they loved helping the kids. However, the one thing that I learned very quickly was that it was a bureaucracy, and with a bureaucracy comes a lot of red tape. I observed that there were a lot of kids in there that had some of the issues that I had when I was a kid: abusive relationships, dysfunctional families, drug-infested environments, and violent neighborhoods. What I observed was that we would bring a child out of a certain environment (the unit was a live-in set up) and they would be helped to overcome their particular problem. We would see their behavioral problems change, and observe that they were back on track to a relatively normal mental state. Then, we would send them right back into that same destructive environment. I would then see some of the same kids come back within a few months. They call these kids "institutionalized children."

There were a lot of dedicated people working there who would pour their hearts out to help these kids, and it was a great learning experience for me, but it also helped me to view the world in a different way. I realized that it wasn't just the kids that needed fixing, it was the world in which they lived, their social environment, their schools, and parents. The issues went far deeper than most could even imagine, and were intangible things that we just couldn't fix in our controlled environment. It was precisely this realization that made me turn my attention away from wanting to be a Psychiatrist. I wanted something that I felt gave me more freedom and that could impact more people on a day-to-day basis.

My experience at the hospital certainly changed me, and even to this day has helped me to look at the bigger picture; the issues behind the issues.

I had some fun experiences on the unit too. I got to know a lot of the kids individually and treated them as such. The kids would often say, "You can't leave, you're just as crazy as us!" They said that because I did unorthodox things while I was there. Instead of treating them with the textbook solution, I would mirror their behavior so that they could see exactly what they were doing in me. I'm not at liberty to go into all of the practices, but there were a few things that I did that worked. The kids could relate to the mirroring, and seemed to respect it in a sense.

Before I left the hospital, something that I also started to do was speak in front of groups. I started speaking in front of small groups, in high school settings, and with other children outside of the hospital. I started talking with kids and adults about some of my experiences and the things that made me successful to date. It was my way of sharing, giving back, and hopefully being that role model that someone was to me in the past.

It was rewarding for me, to be able to share with people. Some of us have intrinsic skills and things that we enjoy, and one of them that still does give me that feeling of purpose is being able to help others; whether it is speaking, or in this particular case writing a book. It makes me feel as though everything that has happened in my life has happened for this particular moment; right here and right now.

CHOICE...

Sharing the concept of choice with the kids is something that I continue to share with people of all ages today. I'm sharing my story with the world now, and maybe it will help someone else to be stronger.

Sharing my story may give someone else the realization that they too have the power of choice. Sharing my story may also give someone the idea that they are responsible for their life; that they are responsible for their actions and reactions. Sharing my story may help someone take responsibility, or should I say "choose" responsibility.

One thing that I like about this whole process of making a choice is that by making a choice YOU maintain control. By giving up responsibility, you give up control in your life. By blaming someone else for your problems, you relinquish control. In my life now, it is important to me that I know that I am self-directed, making choices, and responsible for my choices, actions, and reactions.

That is another reason, or part of the reason why I choose to get up to meditate and practice yoga everyday. I choose to do that everyday because it gives me my own anchor. One thing that I learned is that life is always changing and can be very unstable. I need something to anchor me.

Nothing stays the same in life. Some people want a sense of stability and security. When you walk out of your door every single day, you have no idea what is going to happen to you. For me, it is important to have a stable "rock"; a center for me to hold on to. The interesting thing about this is that this type of stability is very freeing.

MEDITATION

As I mentioned previously, meditation is my medication. Meditation isn't going to be everyone's medication, but it goes back to spending some time alone every single day.

We'll talk later about creating a sacred space for yourself and spending at least one minute there everyday. That place could be your anchor; the one thing that, no matter what, is constant in your life. For me, each day at four AM, when no one is awake, there are no phones ringing, there are no appointments to get to, birds aren't chirping, and it's simply quiet. Before I step out of my front door every day to do what I have planned to do, I have accomplished something. I am successful every single day, because meditating and practicing yoga daily is success to me. I am achieving that goal every day. Everything else is a bonus.

THE BEGINNINGS OF A
MOTIVATIONAL SPEAKER

I loved speaking back when I worked at the hospital. Whenever and wherever I could speak, I would do so. I really enjoyed the experience, and I didn't really realize that it was something that you could make a career out of. That was until a friend's father turned me on to Brian Tracy and I listened to some of his tapes. Since that day over twenty years ago, Mr. Tracy has become one of my virtual mentors. I remember listening to some of his tapes and thinking that it was some of the greatest stuff that I had ever heard.

One of the first tapes that I heard was *The Psychology of Achievement*. He talked about the universal principles, the Law of Attraction, and some other principles that we talked about in the first part of this book. Then, I was turned on to Les Brown, Tony Robbins, and a host of other great minds. Hearing these speakers made me want to do what they were doing, and essentially become a motivational speaker.

As with plenty of other things in life, sometimes we begin to place limits on ourselves. The limits that I placed on myself, which I now see were ludicrous, were that I hadn't done anything "outstanding" in order to be able to motivate someone else. For example, one of Brian Tracy's claims to fame was that he was an outstanding salesman and an outstanding manager. Those were the things that he was really successful at, and I thought, "How am I going to get up there and tell someone else how to be a super successful salesman or manager when I am not one myself?"

Now, twenty years later, I have worked in sales, I have been a manager, and I would say that I've done pretty well as far as making a living at both. What I *can't* really say is that I've been "outstanding" in both, or that those skills were really my strong points.

After much consideration and thought, I realized that

the one thing that anyone who knows me can tell you is that I'm high energy, happy, friendly, and genuinely encouraging... most of the time. I've had my friends and professional colleagues call me for advice and motivation frequently. I've had friends that have said to me "Hey Chappale, I'm getting ready to go and take this test, and I wanted a few positive words from you to get me in the right state of mind" or "Hey Chappale, I'm going in for this job interview, can you coach me so that I come across in the best possible way?"

Encouraging and coaching people is what I am *"outstanding"* at. To be seen in this light is a wonderful thing, and I'm always excited to help and motivate others. I have always said that I want to inspire greatness in myself and others, but I want to do something truly great first. The more I thought about this, the more I thought that maybe my life *is* already a great example.

Just looking at some of the things that I have been through, and how I have what most people want out of life: to be happy. It is a great place to be. I have had and continue to have those things that help make a person truly happy. First and most importantly, I have the awareness and true belief in the power of choice—the power to choose my attitudes and actions. Secondly, my well is overflowing with energy. I am told almost every day by someone that I am the most enthusiastic person that they know.   Finally, I have the awareness of mind to be grateful for everything; the big and the small.

Last but not least, I am successful because I am happy... most of the time. My happiness is genuine. I'm not talking about a fake happiness, I'm talking about being genuinely happy at the core of my being. I'm happy with who I am, I'm happy with the person that I've become, and I'm happy with the person that I am becoming.

As I said at the beginning of this text, if only one person benefits from this book, my mission has been accomplished.

SOMETIMES YOU STRAY FROM THE PATH...

When I was working at the hospital, I started speaking with different organizations. I loved speaking with people, inspiring them, and giving them tools that they could use immediately in their day-to-day lives. It got to the point where I really wanted to become the best that I could be, and improve my stage presence. At that time I went to a college acting teacher and asked for some advice on exercises that I could use to improve my stage presence while doing my speeches. I wanted to articulate better and I wanted to be able to give effective and entertaining presentations.

Well, I got a little bit more than I bargained for! She threw me a script and said, "I have auditions for a play on Tuesday night. I want you to come." I immediately told her that I didn't want to be an actor; I just wanted to increase my stage presence for *speaking*. She replied, "I heard what you said, and I said that we have auditions on Tuesday night. I want you to come." She then proceeded to tell me that the best way to improve my stage presence was to get on stage and perform in a play. She said it with such conviction that I couldn't really argue with her about it.

Tuesday night, I was at the audition, landed a role, and I did exactly what she told me to do. I got on stage and I performed in a play. Well, that was quite an experience, and I'm glad that I was open to it because I had a lot of fun. This was one of my lessons in "being open to new experiences," because what happened thereafter took me on a whole different journey.

THESPIAN

A few months later, I got a telephone call from the same woman who encouraged me to act in the play, Dr. Vernell Lillie of the Kuntu Repertory Theatre. She said "Chappale, I need your help. I need you to perform in another play for me." At the time I was still working a lot of hours at the psychiatric hospital and didn't really have too much time for anything else in my life. I told her that I wouldn't be available for the rehearsals because of my job. She then, once again, twisted my arm into doing it for her. She assured me that I would only have about three lines in the production, and that I would not have to attend all of the rehearsals. She kept her word, and I did two rehearsals.

The first few weeks of the production were very easy, just like she said. I had three lines and I was on and off in less than 60 seconds! This was community theater and it had a lot of moving parts. During the fourth week of the run, one of the lead characters had an emergency business trip and had to drop out of the production. It was so sudden; it wasn't planned and there was no understudy!

Dr. Lillie, as could be expected at this point, pulled me aside and said "I need for you to take over his role." Of course I was reluctant to do it, but I asked her when she needed for me to step in. Again, in true Dr. Lillie fashion, she said, "I need someone for the next show... which is tomorrow." Before I had a chance to protest, she then went on to say, "Well, you've been watching the production for some weeks now; you can do it. I believe in you."

Of course, I thought of all the reasons in the book not to face this fear: "I don't know his lines... I don't know his blocking... we only had one night to prepare..."; the list was endless. She looked me dead in the eye and said, "It's a window of opportunity for you and will be good for your speaking career down the line. Trust me." Well, who was I to argue with that?

That night I stayed up all night with the script, learning the lines. The next day I went on stage and did it. Of course, I made mistakes here and there, but the people in the audience didn't know what was going on. There was one scene where I missed a whole page of the script, and another where the stage manager said, "You're up," and I didn't have a clue as to what he was talking about. I grabbed the script from him, read the line, memorized it, then ran back out on the stage and delivered it with aplomb. The rest of the wonderful cast made accommodations for my foibles.

The whole experience was a real adrenaline rush, and it was at that moment in my life that I thought, "I want to be an actor." Now remember, I began acting because I wanted to improve my motivational speaking skills; that's why I started in the first place. But after that experience, I was bitten by the acting bug and my life then took another interesting turn.

GONE WITH THE WIND

I have always been one of those passionate, impulsive people. When there is something that I want to do, I go and do it. I once heard someone say something that resonated with me:

"Enjoy life. It is not a dress rehearsal."

We're not going to come this way again in this form, at this time, ever again. So, I have made a conscious choice to live a passion-filled life. I think that at the moment in my life when I decided that I wanted to pursue an acting career, I was doing just that: living passionately. I found something else other than motivational speaking that I was passionate about and decided to follow the calling.

So I applied to and was accepted into a Masters program in acting at the University of Pittsburgh. It was then that I decided to leave my job as a therapist at the psychiatric hospital in order to pursue a career in acting. During the time that I was studying acting at Pitt, I applied for a program to go and study acting in Russia and was accepted to the Masters program through Carnegie Mellon University to study at the Moscow Arts Theatre. At the eleventh hour, I had a change of heart about the program and the direction that I was going in. I had been in Pitt's Masters program for a year, had just closed my first professional theatre job at Pittsburgh's City Theatre, and felt ready to take on the challenges and glory of the world of acting. I felt that more studying would prolong my journey to the bright lights of Broadway and the big screen. At the last moment I decided that I was ready to move to The Big Apple and just go for it. Within the next few months, I had packed my bags and moved to New York.

BRIGHT LIGHTS..BIG CITY

New York City was one of the most rewarding experiences of my life. They say that you grow when you step beyond your comfort zone, and I found that to be true every step of the way in my journey to New York. My girlfriend at the time and I both decided to make the move to New York. Moving to NYC and out of my comfort zone was a huge part of my growth into the person that I am today. New York is a melting pot; there are different cultures, different foods, and different languages all swirling in one huge pot. I absolutely loved it, my horizons were widened in so many ways.

When I got there, I found a job with Miramax Films as a first executive assistant in the Marketing Department. Once my girlfriend at the time and I were settled, we decided to start a theater company together. It was called "Just Once a Month." The premise of our company was that we produced theater, small one-person shows, or ten minute play competitions... just once a month. It was one of my first business ventures.

We put our own money into it, did the mailings, and grew the subscription base from just a handful of people to over 600 people in a short period of time. The reason for starting this venture originally was to use it as a vehicle for our careers. It served that purpose for a short period of time. My acting career in New York was slow, but it had its shining moments. One of them was appearing in a national commercial as the lead actor, alongside Ice T. Filming that commercial was just amazing; we were at the famous Apollo Theater for a few days with hundreds of crew members and other dancers and actors. I felt like a king for a few days.

After several years of small parts on independent or student films, and working every spare moment on Just Once a Month, I felt a little stagnated. It was the perfect time to make a change—I was laid off from Miramax films, my girlfriend and I had broken up months before, and Just Once a Month was starting to wear. I lived in New York for about five years and then decided that I needed a change of pace to take my acting to the next level...

CITY OF ANGELS

New York and California are the hubs for actors in the United States. Again, after five years in New York, it started to feel a little cramped for me. I was taking everything that was happening to me as a sign to leave the city and venture into new territory. I had to make myself uncomfortable once again in order to grow. I decided that perhaps it was time to explore the other coast of the United States. It was the perfect time for me to try something new. I believe that life gives you those little signs that it's time to move onto new things, and it's our responsibility to take note of those signs. They are jewels.

Moving to Los Angeles didn't come without its challenges. In New York I did not require a vehicle. It's a "vertical" city; people are in the streets walking, biking, and using the subways. In Los Angeles, which is much more of a horizontal city (more spread out), a car was pretty much a necessity for me, so that was the first thing on my agenda: get a car. A few days prior to my departure, I went to a car auction in Ohio and purchased my pride and joy—a 1991 Plymouth Acclaim for sixteen hundred dollars ($1,600.00).

I had never really spent too much time in Los Angeles, but having exercised that muscle of change regularly in New York and up to that date in my life, it was something that I was certainly looking forward to.

My actual trip to Los Angeles was even more exciting. I love that phrase that goes, "It's not about the destination; it's about the journey." On the way back to New York from Ohio, where I purchased the car, the Plymouth broke down. I was in the middle of the highway with a car that didn't work, and I was going to be driving to Los Angeles in just three days. I couldn't tell any of my friends about the car problems, because none of them would have let me go if they realized that the car I was driving had major issues. I decided that I wasn't going to tell anyone. I would just get in the car and take the trip. Ready or not.

Now, I'm certainly not advocating that anyone do this, because it wasn't the smartest thing to do, however, it was an adventure all in itself to embark upon the journey without being 100% ready for it. I felt that way about writing this book and recording my first audio program. I felt that way when I recorded my first DVD entitled *Creative Ways to Choose Happiness*. Did I feel 100% ready? No, but I decided to feel the fear and do it anyway! Life is to be lived, and if we're always waiting for the perfect time to be 100% ready all of the time, there are so many opportunities that we may miss out on. Sometimes we need to just take a leap of faith!

So I got into my defective car, gave all of my furniture and items away (except for my books, CDs, and a few clothes), and began my trek across the country.

I decided to stop at a few places on the way. My first stop was back in Pittsburgh. I made it to Pittsburgh without any problems, and it was wonderful to see many old friends and reconnect. No matter how busy life gets, I think that it is really important to connect with people from your past who have helped shape you.

Michigan to Chicago was when I started to have a little trouble on the road. Basically, all hell broke loose and my car began to stall. My biological father found a backyard mechanic to help me fix a broken fuel pump. That fixed fuel pump took me across the terrain to Nebraska. When I arrived in Nebraska, the car broke down again on the side of the road and I spent the night in a corn field. Five hundred dollars ($500.00) later, it was fixed. From there I decided to surprise my grandmother (who had moved several years earlier) by dropping in on her in Denver, Colorado. She had no idea that I was moving across the country. I just knocked on her door and spent some quality time there with her for about a week. Then I traveled from Denver to the Grand Canyon.

Now, the Grand Canyon wasn't a part of the original plan, but I felt that since I was so close, it was something that I should do. I was a little afraid, as far as the situation with the car, but I told myself to have the courage to live life and live it to the fullest, right now in the moment. I said, "Don't worry about the future; live in the present." This statement is *not* saying that you should not plan for the future, because I do believe that planning is important. But what this does mean is that you should not *worry* about the future; live in the here and now because the only thing you really have is *this moment*. Right NOW.

I am so glad that I did choose to live in the present at that moment. It was such a great experience, and because of it, I would advise anyone that hasn't seen the Grand Canyon to go. It is an amazing, awesome site. That was the first time I really came to a true understanding of the word AWESOME! I paid just $20.00 for one of the most breathtaking experiences of my life; an encounter that was worth way more than that. It certainly allayed my fears about my car problems. Standing at the tip of the Grand Canyon, witnessing its sheer size and colorful intricate landscape inspired me in a way that I hope I've been able to describe here properly.

After my brief excursion to the canyon, I drove back down from there and went to visit another friend in Arizona. From Arizona, I went straight to California. There were other stories and "side-of-the-road" car adventures, but all and all, it was a wonderful journey. I had time to think about life and reflect while on the open road. I listened to music that inspired me, absorbed the landscapes, different cities and the people—both old and new. I truly took the time out to enjoy my surroundings. My journey in total took about 19 days, and I remember being just a little bit sad when I crossed the California border. I truly learned the lesson during that trip that it is about the journey, and not the destination.

During my journey I met so many wonderful people, saw some great landscapes, and connected with family and old friends. I align this to life in general. We are naturally goal-achieving mechanisms, and goals are obviously extremely important because they give us direction, but we must remember to live in each moment of the journey. The journey is one to be savored, experienced to the fullest, and lived every single moment; both the good and the bad. Goals are great because they give you something to shoot for, but that alone probably won't be enough to make you happy.

Living life fully, being loving, living in the moment, being aware, helping others, making productive choices, and continually being grateful is what has made me so happy.

Think about everything that you have wanted to

achieve in your life. Consider every medal, every goal, every sale, and every accomplishment. It's all about the journey. Even before the New York to California road trip, I learned the lesson about "the journey" in college.

When we won The Big East conference championship, it was a great experience. At that moment in time, however, it was extremely anti-climatic for me. The Big East Championship is what we as a team aspired to winning. At the time of winning, right in the midst of it, I was thinking, "What next?" We were running around the track with our trophy, and I was there thinking, "What next?"

What I came to realize later was that it wasn't the goal that was the most important thing. It was who I became and what I experienced in the process of achieving the goal; that was the most important thing. The journey had brought with it the ability to master intense athletic training, lessons of discipline, the ability to endure aching muscles, long-lasting friendships, arduous weight-training sessions, excruciating endurance exercises, stories from Coach Lewis that have helped me throughout life, lessons in wisdom and preparedness, and the ability to balance track and studying at the same time. All of those elements were part of the journey that culminated in me running around the track with thousands of supporters cheering in the background as we carried that huge, golden trophy.

TO BE OR NOT TO BE....

This book is entitled *How To Choose Happiness... Most of the Time.* The one thing that I have learned along the way is that if you're looking for other people, outside circumstances, or things to make you intrinsically happy, you will be disappointed. That is not the secret. When I say that, there are many who refute my assertion that other people can't make you happy. If you go into a relationship thinking that another person is going to make you happy, I would encourage you to think long and hard about that. No one can make you *intrinsically* happy—you have to choose it for yourself. Someone else can *complement* your happiness, but they can not *make* you happy. I learned that lesson the hard way.

I have been involved with many people who were very unhappy—both friends and romantic interests. I embarked on a quest for their happiness, and thought that I might be able to make them happy by being a good person, saying the right things, and doing nice things for them. I've learned after many years of trying that you may be able to make someone happy momentarily, but you can't *intrinsically* change someone's ability to be happy. They have to *choose* it for themselves. You can't force someone to be happy, no matter how badly you want it for them. People have to deal with their issues themselves, the best way they can. You can assist by being a good listener, recommending a good book, and/or spending quality time with them. However, when it's all said and done, it is about that person taking responsibility and control over their life, and choosing their own actions, reactions, and perspectives.

NEW BEGINNINGS....

I had always been told that California and New York are like night and day. Once I arrived, I had the opportunity to make the assessment for myself.

I was and am still so grateful to have come to California. At first, it was a very big adjustment for me. I remember coming to California and thinking that I was going to become a star overnight... *Look out world, because here I come!*

I met a lot of people from my theatre company in New York, and had a pretty wide network that I thought would really serve me well in Los Angeles. Many people said to me, "Don't worry about anything when you get to L.A., I'll introduce you to this person and that person." I frequently heard those famous last words: "Just give me a call." I thought I was a bit of a mover and shaker in New York; I knew the right people, went to the right events, and was definitely well-connected. I made the presumption that things would be the same in L.A.

So when I got to L.A., I did just as I was told. I made those calls to get connected. Unfortunately, the majority of my calls went unanswered. I was so uncomfortable to begin with, and now on top of that, most of the people who had made certain promises to me were nowhere to be found.

It was not all bad though. There were a few people who went out of their way to help me; one of them was John Murchison and another was Russell Hornsby. I am grateful to them because they helped make my transition a bit smoother. Los Angeles can be a very lonely place for one thing, and it's not a very nice place to need people. I was very fortunate to have a place to stay. My ex-girlfriend's mother lived in L.A., and my ex suggested that I ask her Mom to rent a room. That worked out very well. I am so thankful for that opportunity to this day.

There are some people that you meet along your journey who don't even know how much they're doing for you at certain points in your life. My ex's mother was certainly one of those people. She was like a surrogate mother to me. I rented a room in her house, and each and every day that I was there, she looked out for me. At times, she went above and beyond, making sure that I had fresh fruit to eat every day, and more importantly that I had a warm haven to come home to each evening.

When I first got to Los Angeles, I didn't have a job. I was living off of my savings. I immediately started to take some smaller jobs. I started doing some "extra" work for money. I then decided that the best way to start networking for my acting career was to start taking classes.

BACK TO BASICS...

One of the first classes that I was introduced to was the "Image Design Class" by Sam Christensen. The class was in a stylish studio in North Hollywood. The purpose of the class was to help people understand how others view them. It gave me a clear and accurate picture of how the world saw me, and how that in turn could help me redefine who I was as it related to my acting career, in terms of casting and designing my image. The end goal of the class was to come up with seven essences that described me. To get to that point after seven weeks, there was a lot of soul-searching, surveying, and reading that I needed to do.

At the end of the class I had to do a scene where I posted my essences up for the audience to see. Then I had to figure out what my purpose was. Here is the actual list of my essences:

MY ESSENCES
Full of Life
A Gentleman by Choice
I Get a Little Intense
A Great Big Kid
I Care
Happy
The Desire for Greatness

360 DEGREES

Through my participation in this course I had a revelation. This whole class, the introspection, and the time that I spent with Mr. Christensen talking and deliberating over my true desires brought me right back in a big circle to my original purpose; 360 degrees. My purpose was and is: To Inspire Greatness in Myself and In Others. (Greatness for me is truly living your best life. Doing the best that you can do and being true to yourself in the process. It's different for everyone and only you know when you are truly doing your best. The interesting thing is that the more you do your best, the better you become, hence the target keeps moving and you keep growing.

Once again, it's really about the journey and not the destination, so you may as well enjoy the process.)

This was really funny to me because I was in that class to learn how to become a better actor, and instead I had that revelation. I began acting initially because I went to Dr. Lillie to become a better speaker. I started out wanting to be a motivational speaker—*not* an actor. So there I was in an acting class that was taking me right back to the motivational speaking.

I'd gotten a little side-tracked from my very first goal, but here I was right back where I originally wanted to be. I could have been annoyed with myself, but I really wasn't. I was actually grateful for the experiences that I had enjoyed up to that date, because all of them would eventually help me to help others through my speaking. You've got to have a story to tell.

Right at that point in time, I stopped taking the class. I thanked my instructor and told him that I wouldn't be signing up for the next class. I let him know that I really loved acting, and that I might do it again sometime in the future, but that I had re-realized that my purpose was intended for something else. Now, that is not to suggest that I couldn't inspire people through film, theatre, movies, and television, but I would most likely be playing other characters and not myself. I realized at that point that it was through my stories, and just being Chappale, that I would be able to inspire others. That was how I was going to further my purpose:

"To Inspire Greatness in Myself And Others"

NEW DIRECTIONS

Sometimes in life, you have to re-evaluate what you're doing and adjust your direction if necessary. It's okay if you have to do that. At that point in my life, which was about eight years ago, I decided that it wasn't acting that I really wanted to do; I wanted to be a motivational speaker. I wanted to help people in their day-to-day lives.

Well, I had been doing part-time jobs during my initial introduction to Los Angeles, like extra work and odd jobs here and there. The next full-time job I got after my epiphany, was one as a security guard for a company now called Securitas. So here I was in California, making $7.75 per hour, driving a 1991 Plymouth Acclaim, and as happy as I could be because I was working towards a new goal. I thoroughly enjoyed my experience as a security guard — it was a long way from the executive suites of Miramax, but I learned some things about myself and others in the process.

I remember L.A. was the first place I came to where one of the first things certain people (especially women) would ask was "What do you drive?" It was interesting to me that people wouldn't ask me about myself, my interests, or my dreams before asking what I drive! It was then interesting to see people's faces when I answered them. It was a funny experience, especially when I told them with such pride.

My job was far from glamorous. I was making an honest living—not a great deal of money, but an honest living. I remember when I told people that I was a security guard, I could see their faces change, and some of them would have nothing further to say to me. I never had those types of issues in New York, which was strange to me. The lesson that I learned here was one about the "Ego." I talk a little bit more about the Ego on my DVD *Creative Ways To Choose Happiness*. I was just as happy then as I am now driving my current luxury vehicle; I'm just more comfortable. It's great to have air-conditioning as an option—especially in Los Angeles.

The reason why is because I have an attitude of nonattachment. I love having nice things, but I'm not attached to them. I don't use my car to define my identity. I didn't when I was driving the rusted-out '91 Acclaim, and I don't now with my current vehicle.

I was actually quite disturbed that people would have such an acerbic reaction to me because of my profession and what I drove. I then realized that those weren't the type of people that I wanted to deal with. If they didn't want to get to know who I was, where I came from, or what my hopes and dreams were for the future, I didn't want any part of them. So from then on, I would make sure that the first things I told people when they asked about me were 1) my car type, 2) my job title, and 3) how much I made (which was $7.75 per hour).

I was pleasantly surprised when I first met my wife. When she asked me what I did for a living, I told her immediately.

"So, what do you do?" she asked.

"I'm a security guard, and I make seven dollars and seventy five cents per hour," I answered her.

She then replied, "Okay, but what do you *do*?"

"I secure the area, observe, and report."

Her response afterwards was so refreshing. She then started to ask me about who I was, and what was "the essence of me." Not my job, not my car, but who *I* was. We then started to have a conversation about our likes and dislikes. Afterwards, we went for breakfast, and the rest is history.

As I stated before, I enjoyed being a security guard. I met some good, hard-working people while doing so. I was exposed to a whole new world, and that might not have been the case if I'd taken a different path. At the company where I worked, one of the area VPs at the time took a special interest in me, and I went from a security guard to an account manager, from an account manager to an HR manager, from an HR manager to a branch manager, and from a branch manager to a business development manager. These developments all occurred in less than five years.

Once back in the corporate world, I started working on my speaking again. I became a certified personal trainer and joined Toastmasters International while continuing to excel in my job at Securitas. Toastmasters International is a non-profit organization that assists people who want to grow and develop through public speaking and leadership.

There are Toastmasters groups all over the world that continue to help thousands of people on a weekly basis to improve their public speaking skills. Some people want to improve their speaking skills for their jobs, to create better communication with colleagues, or to simply improve their skills for leadership opportunities within their communities. It's just a wonderful group, and I am so grateful for what Toastmasters has done for me. It was at Toastmasters that my desire to become a professional motivational speaker grew stronger.

During my time there (as of this writing I have now reached the Advanced Toastmaster Bronze Level) I realized how I was helping people through my speeches on self-development. I then realized that I was affecting people in my close circle with my message about ways in which they could choose happiness. I went on to work as an executive recruiter for several years, and during that time I would coach individuals who also stood to benefit from my teachings. My wife and I still attend weekly Toastmasters meetings to maintain our fire for public speaking.

WHY I WROTE THIS BOOK

One day while meditating at the beach, I realized that I could help so many more people outside of just my close community. That is why I chose to write this book. I believe that I have come a long way from the ghettos of Chicago, and if my story and techniques can help a few more people in this world, then my goal here has been achieved.

I look at myself in the mirror each day and just smile. I smile because I am so grateful. I am so thankful for the situations, people, and things that I have attracted into my life. I am grateful, and I still take the time to just "be." I have chosen happiness, and I am challenging anyone who is reading this book to do the same thing. You now have an example and many tools to use. So be loving, be grateful, embrace life, live it to the fullest, and most importantly CHOOSE HAPPINESS NOW!

Here is your 30 day action plan. It will get you started on the road to being truly happy... most of the time.

30 WAYS IN 30 DAYS WITH 30 ACTION STEPS TO HELP MAKE HAPPINESS A HABIT

In the next pages you will find 30 very specific ways that you can take actions towards "happiness as a habit" in 30 days.

These 30 days are in no particular order. Remember, this is your book and your plan; you can do each day in the order that they're laid out here, or you can do the action steps in the order that suits your lifestyle. Also remember that just reading the steps is not enough. You have to DO the action steps! So, grab something to write with. You can either use a journal or just write directly in this book (if you own it of course) in the composition style notes area at the end of each section. Alright then, let's get going!

DAY 1
DAILY PHYSICAL ACTIVITY "PLAY"—EVERY DAY

Physical activity is a very important action step that can contribute to your overall happiness and wellbeing. When you look and feel good, many areas of your life are positively enhanced. For example, your confidence and energy levels increase. I suggest that you perform some type of physical activity on a daily basis.

What I would like you to realize is that physical activity can be *any productive* activity that you enjoy. There are many people who enjoy going to the gym every day or on a regular basis. There are some people that like to get up every day and run several miles. If you're one of those people, that's fantastic, keep it up! But if you're not, then that is okay also. There are some people who don't like a regular routine and want to do something a little more creative. You can do ANYTHING.

Go for a long walk, play with your kids, play soccer, practice martial arts, swim, roller-blade; anything that will maintain an ideal fitness level. There are other small things that you can add into your daily routine that don't require a lot of effort or planning. You've probably heard the one about finding the furthest parking spot when shopping, going to work, and running errands. Just that small activity can work wonders, and adds just a little bit more physical activity into your daily routine. How about taking the stairs instead of an elevator? Or instead of going through a drive through to get your food, get out of the car and walk inside! How about hiding your remote control for the television, and every time you want to change the channel, you have to get up and change it! All small yet productive ways to add physical activity into your day.

Examples of Daily Physical Activity "Play"

1. Take the stairs instead of the elevator when possible.
2. Park your car further away than normal.
3. Take a 15 minute power walk during your lunch break.
4. Play a "pick-up" game of basketball.
5. Instead of emailing at work, walk over to that person's office or desk when possible.
6. Practice good posture at all times, such as when you are sitting at your desk or the dinner table.
7. Practice breathing properly with your diaphragm.
8. Practice holding your core (abdominal area) in at all times.
9. Do isometric exercises (strength training using

static contractions) whenever possible.

10. Play with your children.

11. Play Frisbee.

12. Play Hopscotch.

13. Join a running or walking club.

14. Take a hike.

15. Take a swim.

16. Go bowling with a friend.

17. Play a couple rounds of golf, and walk the course instead of using a golf cart.

18. Play tennis.

19. Take a Yoga class.

20. Walk in the mall.

21. Walk on the beach or in a park.

22. Go dancing.

23. Go rollerblading.

24. Go for a bike ride.

25. If you take a train to work, walk to the end of the platform.

26. When possible, take trains instead of cabs (it requires more walking, standing, and physical activity in general).

27. Walk to a bus stop that is further down the road.

28. Walk to get lunch or dinner instead of ordering in.

29. Join a local gym with group exercise classes.

30. Carry baskets at the grocery store instead of pushing a cart.

31. Use cleaning your house as a form of exercise (ala Karate kid); put some great music on while you do your housework.

32. Wash your own car instead of going through a drive-thru car wash or detail shop.

33. Do the lawn work and gardening yourself (pushing a lawn mower is good exercise!).

34. When you're sitting at your desk or standing in line at the post office, do some calve raises.

35. Skip rope.

Although all of these things sound like small things, they can add up.

You can maintain your activity level and have fun at the same time. That's why I like to call it "daily activity *play*" instead of exercise, because people generally look forward to playing. The key is to be consistent and enjoy it. When you take the chore out of the activity, you make it fun and maintain your fitness and energy levels at the same time.

<u>DAY 1 ACTION STEP</u>

Write down several activities that you will start today. You can alternate them, or you can do the same thing; it's up to you. The key is consistency. Perhaps you can start today with just one or two activities. Make the commitment to actually do the things that you write down for the next 21 days, and you will have started a habit that will increase your circulation, energy level, self-esteem, and confidence, as well as your overall physical comfort and well being. Good luck.

DAY 2
NIGHTLY GRATEFUL LIST

I spoke about being grateful earlier; you can never be too grateful. I have always been grateful at different points in my life, like at Thanksgiving, or when a near miss happens. However, to be consistently grateful on a daily basis is something completely different. As mentioned earlier, I learned a great method from Oprah Winfrey on this subject—an exercise that she does every night before she goes to bed. She writes out five things that she is grateful for.

I have been doing this for many years now. It has an amazing effect. Something else that happens is that you will start going through your day finding things to be thankful for. In the beginning you have a lot of big things to be grateful for, but as time goes on you'll tap into the smaller things in your life that you may not have even noticed before. You'll start being grateful for both the big and the small things. You'll begin to get a little more in tune with yourself, your life, and your environment when you are grateful for what you have. It makes you a lot more aware. There are things that I took for granted before that I have found myself becoming more and more grateful for. For example, hearing the birds chirp, having a nice hot shower in the morning, drinking a warm cup of tea, or watching the squirrels play outside my door.

Keep a journal next to your bed and start your "grateful" list tonight.

Begin listing things to be grateful for. Start with just five things, and you'll probably find that over time your list will become longer and more detailed.

Another component that you can add to this exercise is to start reading the things that you wrote down the night before first thing the next morning. You'll find that if you do this you will start your day with a smile, or at the very least with a positive disposition.

Examples:
I am thankful for...
1. The hot shower that I was able to take this morning.
2. The food that I ate today.
3. My actions as they pertained to a particular individual.
4. All the money I have right now.
5. The conversation that I had with my friend today.
6. My family.
7. My car that took me to work today.
8. My job.
9. The warm smile that I received from the bank

teller today.

10. The compliment that I received about my new hair style.

DAY 2 ACTION STEP

Stop reading this book for a moment and go place a pen and a journal or a piece of paper on your pillow right now.

Don't go to sleep tonight until you've written five things you are grateful for.

Repeat this action again for the next 21 days until you create a grateful habit.

You'll probably find yourself sleeping better too!

_____

_____

_____

_____

_____

_____

_____

www.MondaySmiles.com

DAY 3

<u>LOOK FOR OPPORTUNTIES TO GIVE</u>

Look for opportunities to give or share with those around you. I started being aware of the need to be more giving by reading a very small book by Deepak Chopra called *Creating Affluence*. I picked up this book because I was looking for a way to create more abundance in my life. But as time went on I noticed other things happening as I digested the information presented in Chopra's book. I started feeling a little more relaxed in certain situations.

For example, in the past, whenever I entered a location where someone was panhandling or asking for money for personal reasons or for a charity, I would tense up. I would try not to make eye contact, or look for another way to enter the store I was visiting. The other thing that I would do is see if I could create a decoy! A decoy operation is when I would wait until someone else was walking into the store and then I would walk alongside them into the store at the same time, so that the panhandling individual wouldn't have a chance to speak to me. You may have seen this happen, and you may have even done it yourself. Right?

But after practicing the principles of giving that I learned in Chopra's book for a while, I now get excited at opportunities to give at every opportunity that I can. Chopra says in his book that you don't always have to give money; you could give a kind word or a smile. If you do have money and feel comfortable giving it away, then by all means do it. By giving away money, you are only affirming your own abundance.

Find opportunities to give sincere compliments. If you want someone to feel really special, give them the gift of your undivided attention.

Examples of ways to give:
1. Donate your old or unused clothes to charity or to someone else you know that needs them.
2. Give someone a sincere compliment.
3. Buy someone a good book or CD.
4. Give someone a sincere smile.
5. Offer some of your time to help a friend complete a project.
6. Bake something for your co-workers for no reason at all.
7. Contribute to a charity.
8. Give encouragement whenever you can.
9. Lend your ear to someone in need.

DAY 3 ACTION STEP

Grab your pen and write down some ways that you plan to give, or just what you plan to give at the next opportunity that presents itself. Sometimes I put a few extra dollars in my pocket, either to give to someone asking for it, or to simply over tip someone that helps me. Don't always look for a "Thank you" either; remember that you're giving for the sake of giving, not for a pat on the back.

_____

_____

_____

_____

_____

_____

_____

_____

www.MondaySmiles.com

DAY 4
LIST THINGS ABOUT YOURSELF

Sometimes we need a confidence boost, and I've found an excellent way to take a positive self-inventory and feel good about yourself: write lists about your strengths and positive attributes. There are three simple lists that I've come up with that I find very useful:

1. List any three things that you like about yourself.
2. List any three things that you do well.
3. List any three things that someone else has said they like about you.

Examples:

1. I like the way I treat people, the way I smile, and my sense of humor.
2. I listen to other people well, I am really organized at home and work, and I play tennis well.
3. I've been told by someone that they like the way I dress, that I have kind eyes, and that I'm a good cook.

Listing three items is just the starting point; you have to start somewhere. Feel free to make this list as long as you'd like.

Keep this list in a journal if that would be helpful for you. Some people are very visual and need to see things written down—you have to do whatever will help you maintain and draw a benefit from these action steps. You can refer to these lists as often as you like. There is no characteristic too small, too big, or too silly to put on these lists. Have fun with it!

I also learned another trick from author and speaker Brian Tracy. It is a good confidence building technique; similar to the affirmations we discussed earlier. Basically, you look in the mirror and repeat the following simple phrase with enthusiasm and feeling:

"I like myself, I like myself, I like myself!"

You can add to this by using items from your lists. For example, "I love the way that I put my clothes together" or "I love the way I am able to complete a project on time." You can be as creative as you like. This is to be a private and personal exercise that no one has to know about except for you. However, if you practice this regularly people will definitely notice you becoming more confident. When your self-worth grows it is very evident to others around you.

DAY 4 ACTION STEP

Start with three things that you like about yourself and feel free to add to this list as often and as much as you like. For the next 21 days read this list over at least three to ten times or more per day. When you read this list, don't just read it with a humdrum, monotone voice. Read it with feeling, enthusiasm, and purpose. Really allow yourself to *feel* those feelings. Smile, breath deeply, and fully engage yourself in what you are doing. It's so important to be 100% conscious of what you are doing here.

One other thing: respect this list. Keep it in a secret and private place. You can think of it as a sacred ritual if that helps, but whatever you do make it special and respect the process.

_____

_____

_____

_____

_____

_____

_____

_____

_____

_____

_____

_____

_____

_____

_____

_____

_____

_____

_____

www.MondaySmiles.com

DAY 5
CREATE THE FUTURE YOU NOW

Look, act, dress, and carry yourself like the person you wish to be. If you want more, be more! Start to study the lives and habits of your heroes, role models, and other people that you admire. You can do this wherever you are and with whatever you have. The public library is still free! No matter what position you're in and no matter where you are, you can always assume greater responsibility and take more control over your life and your attitudes.

Let's say that one of your goals is to become the CEO of a company. Then you have to study the lives, methods, and thought processes of every CEO you come across. Start right now by being the CEO of your own personal world. Begin to take ownership and pride in all of your work. Find ways to create and add more value in your "company," which is your life. Assume that role of CEO and use common sense—or better yet, use *un*common sense. You want to do something out of the ordinary in your life.

Now, don't take this idea the wrong way. In no way do I mean go to work and start bossing people around as if you have power over them. I mean that you want to start being the CEO of *yourself*.

How did other CEOs grow themselves? Find out, and don't wait; start right now. First begin with your attitude. Never be a "that's not my job" type of person. If you take true ownership over yourself and the situation, there is no job too small.

Look the Part

What is your daily disposition and attitude? How do you handle stress? Are you a person that handles it well? Or are you a person that cracks at the first sign of pressure? Most really good CEOs actually look *forward* to problems; they simply look at problems as challenges to overcome and they are happy to do it. They know the value in reframing a "problem" as a "challenge," and challenges excite them. They are happy to take on responsibilities, which is why they are the big bosses and make the big money!

Act "As If"

Sometimes you want to ask yourself the question, "What would a successful CEO do in this situation?" Then, if appropriate, act accordingly. People also respond to the image you project, so be sure to project an image of confidence, leadership, and PURPOSE.

Dress Like a Leader

When I say dress like a leader, it doesn't always mean going out and buying a whole new wardrobe. Sometimes it could be something as simple as ironing your clothes, perhaps taking them to the dry cleaners instead of washing them in the machine, shining your shoes, and paying attention to other visual details. When people see that you take pride in your appearance, they will take you more seriously. Think about it—if you walked into a sales meeting with someone wearing a wrinkled shirt, scuffed shoes, and unkempt hair, would you take them seriously? Or would you think twice about entrusting them with your money?

Carry Yourself as the Person You Wish to Be

Finally, when you are creating the future you now, you have to carry yourself as the person you wish to be. You'll probably never find a CEO gossiping, wasting time, or playing computer games on company time. There are many ways to create the future *you* right now. Be creative.

It goes back to the same principles we discussed earlier: knowing what you want, believing you can have it, creating a plan, and taking action steps. Remember of course to always be flexible.

<u>DAY 5 ACTION STEP</u>

In your journal write a full, detailed description of the person you see yourself becoming. Think of all of the positive character traits that you can come up with and write them down in your journal. Then pick one, two, or three of these traits and create an action plan of how you can incorporate them into your personality.

Over the next 21 days and beyond, start to incorporate these character traits into your personality. Re-evaluate every 21 days and add another two or three positive characteristics to your personality.

_____

_____

_____

_____

_____

_____

_____

_____

www.MondaySmiles.com

DAY 6
CREATE A SACRED SPACE
FOR YOURSELF

{Exist. if fut/ Ideal?}

Everyone needs a place where they can be alone, with no disruptions, stress, or drama; someplace where they can reflect on life, meditate, and evaluate their quest for personal happiness. We will call this a "sacred space."

Create a room, an area, or even just a corner of a room that you can consider a sacred space. It could be as small as a table with items on it that are important to you, or even a shoe box with a few precious items in it. The items don't have to have any monetary value, but they should have some emotional or spiritual value to you. The items could be photos of people that are important to you, or of places that you would like to visit. You can place charms, medallions, inspirational books, and quotes in your shoe box. Anything that can inspire you would be found in this box. It could be a special gift, or a rock that you found on a special day. Your sacred space could be a place that you burn incense, or where you can place fresh flowers and fruit regularly. It doesn't matter what it is, as long as this place is special to you.

60 Seconds

Once you've created your space, you'll want to

respect it, and visit it daily. This is a great space where you will go and reflect on life, meditate, pray, think, visualize, review your goals, and just sit in silence. Any of these activities are good. Ensure that you visit your space for at least 60 seconds a day, up to or even longer than one hour.

Visit your sacred space daily—always make time— and when you're there be conscious, aware, and acutely in the moment. Start off with a visit at least once per day, preferably in the morning before you begin your day. I don't care how busy you are, you can take 60 seconds to center yourself, review items on your list(s), and visualize how you want your day to go. Tell yourself that you are worth investing at least one minute per day into your health and happiness, and make a promise to yourself to actually do so. Don't kid yourself by saying "I just don't have the time." That is just an excuse. Start with 60 seconds!

The key is to make this a daily habit. Those 60 seconds are going to be over before you know it. The next thing you know you're going to find yourself investing more time into yourself. Actually, it takes a few seconds for you to get into your space, and then another 60 seconds to perform your actions—is that such a great sacrifice to make for the sake of your happiness? I know it isn't.

So make a commitment to yourself that you will

invest those 60 seconds for the next 21 days. You're only committing to about one minute a day. If you can convince yourself to do this once a day, 21 days in a row, you will create a habit. Your time in your sacred space will eventually grow. After 21 days, feel free to add a second session in the evening or sometime before bed. In your second session, you may want to mentally review your day. Ask yourself three questions:

1. What could I have done better today?
2. What did I do well today?
3. What am I thankful for?

DAY 6 ACTION STEP

Identify your space and pick a time that you will visit it. Right now. You only need one minute and one corner of a room to start, so there's no excuse.

You can make your space more elaborate as time goes on; just get started with something simple for now!

DAY 7

MAKE A COMMITMENT

You must be committed to your goals if you want them to come to fruition. When you make a commitment, stick to it. Make your word actually mean something. Be a person that does what they say they're going to do; it's great to be known as a man or woman that takes his or her word seriously. The more you do what you say that you're going to do, the more trust and confidence others will have in you, and the more trust and confidence you will have in yourself. A confident person is usually a happier person.

I believe in building muscles one step at a time, so start out with small basic commitments and work your way up to more challenging ones. Let your word be something that you and other people can count on.

DAY 7 ACTION STEP

If you agree, write the following commitments (one, two, or all three) in your journal. But only write this in your journal if you are willing to make the commitment.

1. I (<u>YOUR NAME</u>) am committed to taking responsibility for my thoughts, attitudes, and actions.

2. I (<u>YOUR NAME</u>) am committed to my own personal growth and development, and being the

best person I can be at this moment in time.

3. I (<u>YOUR NAME)</u> am committed to completing this program and all of the action steps that add value to my life.

_____

_____

_____

_____

_____

_____

_____

_____

_____

_____

www.MondaySmiles.com

DAY 8
MAKE A DREAM DIARY OR
A DREAM BOARD

A dream diary is a collection of pictures, words, photographs, artifacts or anything that you feel will inspire or remind you of your dreams. You can be as creative as you like when you are creating your dream diary.

Some people like to get a scrapbook and add images as they go along. I made mine into a collage of images on one large poster board—something I like to call a "dream board." When I completed mine, I framed it and placed it in a place where I could see it daily. I still have it to this day and I still enjoy looking at it. I have photographs and pictures on my dream board of people who I admire, items that I would like to acquire, places where I would like to travel to, and inspiring quotes. I even have "value" words; words like "family" and "love." This is your own special creation, which can have a positive effect on your emotional state.

Having this tool can help motivate you and remind you of what you're working towards. I created my board in 2003 and I have accomplished at least six or more things on it so far, including buying one of my dream cars, taking a trip to Egypt to see the pyramids, and completing a marathon. I don't share this to brag, I offer it as proof that it has worked for me and it can work for you too. Sometimes just glancing over at your dream diary or board will give you a quick dose of inspiration.

DAY 8 ACTION STEP

You can be as creative as you'd like with this fun exercise. Start to compile images, quotes, items, and things that inspire you. Put them together in a format that pleases you. You can brainstorm and write them here or in your journal.

Review this compilation daily and feel those feelings of having what you want and desire in life. Viewing these images daily also helps to plant them firmly into your subconscious mind magnetizing them into your reality.

Be in the moment; not just wishing for, but truly experiencing the feelings of having what you want right now. This really works if you feel the feelings of having what you want!

_____

_____

_____

_____

_____

_____

www.MondaySmiles.com

DAY 9
EMBRACE FAILURE AND CHOOSE
NOT TO BE PERFECT

If you tell someone to embrace failure and choose imperfection they may look at you sideways. This idea may seem counter intuitive—why would someone ever embrace failure?

Well, when you take a closer look at it, failure can be a short cut to success. By failing more you're actually eliminating options that don't work, which will get you closer to the ones that do. In the process of failing, you gain several things including experience and knowledge of how *not* to do something. You also build the mental fortitude and strength of character that it takes to succeed in the face of a difficult situation.

It has been said that Thomas Edison failed 10,000 times when he was inventing the light bulb. Colonel Sanders failed over 1,000 times while trying to sell his chicken recipe. Michael Jordan, the basketball legend, failed a lot more than he succeeded in order to become one of the greatest basketball players in the world!

Does a baby give up after trying to walk the first time? No, a baby keeps failing and failing until one day he or she is able to walk, and then eventually run. If you're comprehending these words, you have overcome failure many times. And you will do so again and again. You did it when you learned to speak and then understand English.

So face your failures and embrace them with both arms. Hug them tightly. Create visuals of your success and look forward to failure; make it a part of your process. Make your action plan and feel the feelings of having what you want. Then fail, fail some more, do, do again, do some more, be flexible, and fail some more. Eventually your success will come. It was Henry Ford that said, "Failure is simply the opportunity to begin again, this time more intelligently."

The second part of this formula is choosing not to be perfect. Personally, I can admit that I have been guilty of "analysis paralysis." What that means is that I'm so busy analyzing the situation at hand that I sometimes don't get things done as quickly as I would like to.

For example, one of my issues has been waiting for the perfect time to complete this book. I wanted it to be perfect and to give you every bit of information I could. I finally figured out that the book is never going to be perfect, and that if I kept waiting for it to be perfect, it would never get done. I realized that if I had the right intentions, put the words down on paper, and remained open and flexible to constructive feedback that I could produce something that may assist others in achieving their goals. There may be a few things in this book that will be improved upon in future editions, but the most important thing is that it's complete and that I did the best that I could at this given moment in time. Additionally, I know that my intentions are pure. I love the phrase that Nike made famous... "JUST DO IT!!!"

Without a doubt, nothing gets done unless you take an action. Get over your obsession with perfection and do the best you can with what you have at this moment in time. As you grow and continue to take action, you will gain more skills and more experience, which will ultimately strengthen your courage and your ability to perform.

DAY 9 ACTION STEP

Choose three things that you are going to be okay with failing at. For example, if you choose to learn a language, be okay with failing at saying things correctly. If you're going to pick up an instrument, be okay with sounding off and making horrible sounds at first. While you're out there failing and pursuing your dreams and goals, someone else is out there sitting on the sidelines wishing that they had the courage to even try.

_____

_____

_____

_____

_____

_____

_____

_____

_____

_____

_____

_____

_____

_____

DAY 10
LOOK AT THE WORLD THROUGH THE EYES
OF A HAPPY PERSON

Here is a very fun game that you can play with yourself. Use this game to choose your emotional state.

First, think about the happiest person that you can imagine. This can be a real person that you know personally, it can be an actor, or it can be someone that you create in your mind. Once you get a good mental image of that person in your mind, begin to study them. How does this person walk? How do they talk? How do they stand? How do they interact with other people? What is it that makes them happy most of the time? After you've done a good study of this person, close your eyes. When you re-open them, pretend for a few moments (or as long as you like) that you can see the world the way they see things. Just pretend for a moment that you can overlook the flaws of others. Pretend that you can find something good to learn from every situation. Pretend that everything happens for a reason to your benefit, even if you don't know why. Pretend that everyone likes you and wants to be around you. Just pretend that you are happy right now, where you are, with what you have.

What did you learn from playing this little game? How do you feel?

<u>DAY 10 ACTION STEP</u>

Do this now. Write at least three productive things in your journal that you would do differently if you were the happiest person that you knew.

Now over the next 21 days, do those things. Remember when I told you to act "as if."

_____

_____

_____

_____

_____

_____

_____

_____

_____

_____

_____

www.MondaySmiles.com

DAY 11
LIVE A LIFE OF NO REGRETS

Live a life of no regrets. Overcoming your doubts and fears helps to make life special and exciting. Each time you attempt to overcome a challenge you grow as a person. Take a chance on your wildest dreams no matter what they are. Whatever your dream is, find a way to accomplish it, or simply be a part of it.

I'm not saying to quit your job, move to New York City, and become a fashion designer (if that happens to be your dream). There are ways to take baby steps so that you can ease into your dream.

Start right where you are. If it is fashion design, take a class. Design or make something and sell it on EBay, at a yard sale, or to a friend. If your interest is acting, take a class, join a community theater group, and/or act in a small theater production. If it's travel you love, go to a bookstore or a library and look at travel guides. Plan a small trip and grow from there. Start to budget for your trip so that it can be become a reality. Do something each day to see yourself in that particular place where you'd like to be. Live your dreams. Visualize and see yourself there. Listen to the ocean, feel the wind on your face. If it's skiing, feel yourself skiing down that slope.

Whatever your dream is, there is a way that you can begin today, in this moment, to make it happen.

<u>DAY 11 ACTION STEP</u>

In your journal, write three small steps you can take towards the life you would love to create. Do at least one of these actions today.

It could be doing research on the Internet, making a phone call, or sending a letter. Whatever it is, do it within 24 hours of your reading of this action step.

_____

_____

_____

_____

_____

_____

_____

_____

_____

www.MondaySmiles.com

DAY 12
GO WINDOW/EXPERIENCE SHOPPING!

Window shopping, or "experience shopping" as I like to call it, can be an exciting experience! It can make you happy and optimistic about what will happen for you in the future. First create a list of anything that you want, then go window shopping. If it is an activity, go and experience it by observing. Whatever it is that you want—a suit, a television, or a car—go and try it on for size. Experience the feeling of owning it, just for those few moments. This can really help to intensify your visualization sessions as well.

If it's an expensive dress that you want, try it on and enjoy the way the material feels against your body. If it is a car that you like, go to the showroom, test drive the car, and see it as yours. You have to allow yourself to experience owning it. Convince yourself that the item is already yours; you're just going to leave it there in the store for a moment, and they're going to look after it until you're ready to come back and purchase it. Have fun with this exercise; play and enjoy it. Make a game out of it.

If you have an open-minded friend, maybe it's a good idea to take them along with you. Maybe you can both try each other's dreams out for size. Now *that* is a great way to enjoy a Saturday afternoon.

Examples of Window or Experience Shopping:

1. Take a surfing lesson.
2. Go to your nearest showroom and test drive or sit in the car of your dreams.
3. Take a cooking class .
4. Try on, or go look at a piece of expensive jewelry.
5. Take a salsa dancing class.
6. Go to an open house for the house of your dreams.
7. Go to a musical instrument store and try an instrument on for size.
8. Take a helicopter ride.
9. Go race car driving for a day.
10. Attend an Expo – Car, Health, Book, Inventions, Yoga, etc.

DAY 12 ACTION STEP

Set a date to go to an open house, go window shopping, test drive a car, visit a yoga studio, take a Capoeira class, or anything that you want to experience or try. Start with one experience, and let your plans develop from there. Set a date and do it now.

DAY 13
DO KIND THINGS FOR OTHERS

Being kind and thoughtful to others is actually a gift to yourself. Think about how you feel just after you've done something kind or wonderful for another person. It makes you feel great, and you think, why didn't I do that sooner!

Just come up with a list of kind things you can do for others in your life. However, it doesn't absolutely have to be on a list; it could be something that is spontaneous.

Doing kind things for others can become a habit; a good one at that. Even if it sounds selfish that you're doing kind things for others so that you will feel good, then so what? Do it anyway. At least two people are ultimately getting something out of it. What a great way to be selfish and be proud of it! You can say it with pride: **I help people because it makes me feel good**.

Examples of kind things you can do for others:
1. Give an anonymous gift.
2. Put money in a parking meter that is about to expire.
3. Over tip for good service from your waiter, waitress, bellman, barista, or valet.
4. Leave a tip for the housekeeping staff at a hotel.

134

5. Be the friendliest and most genuine person you know.

6. Call someone just to tell them that you're thinking about them.

7. Leave everything better than you found it.

8. Tell someone that they're doing or have done a good job.

9. Let someone know that you appreciate them.

10. Pay the toll for the car behind you.

DAY 13 ACTION STEP

Decide which three or more acts of kindness you can take, and do them this week. Once you've done this a few times, you'll probably find yourself looking for other ways to be kind to people.

_____

_____

_____

_____

_____

www.MondaySmiles.com

DAY 14
LISTEN TO OR WATCH SELF
DEVELOPMENT PROGRAMS

In your quest for a fulfilling life, you want to begin to watch or listen to positive information, such as self-development programs that are interesting to you. There is so much great information in audio and visual format that there is absolutely no excuse for not continuing in your self-development and personal growth.

I was listening to a Brian Tracy audio once and he said, "Turn your car into a university on wheels." Having audio programs playing in your car not only makes the travel time go much quicker, it also causes you to be a little bit more productive with your time as well. When you're sitting in traffic and listening to a self-development audio program, you don't mind the wait so much.

On some occasions I have been in my car enjoying an audio program and reached my destination so fast that I actually chose to sit in my car a little bit longer so that the audio program could finish.

The more I listen, the more I learn. And the more you play these educational/inspirational CDs and DVDs, the more the messages become a part of you and your thought process. So, when negative or unhappy thoughts enter your mind the way they sometimes do, you'll have more tools to counteract them.

Recommended Audio/DVD Programs:

· *Creative Ways to Choose Happiness* – Chappale Linn Burton
· *The Psychology of Achievement* – Brian Tracy
· *Live Your Dreams* – Les Brown

DAY 14 ACTION STEP

Locate a library that has audio programs that you can borrow or invest in a self-development program that you can buy at a bookstore or on the Internet. Find one that sounds interesting to you, and listen to it in your car as you drive to work or to other destinations.

If you don't have a car, then no problem; improvise. Listen to your programs on a headset as you ride the bus, train, or walk. Of course, you should always be safe and maintain alertness, as you can easily get so wrapped up in the awesome messages in self-development CDs that you may lose awareness of your surroundings. Write the name of your first audio program here.

_____

_____

DAY 15
STUDY PSYCHOLOGY

We're at Day 15—excellent! You've made it to the halfway mark.

On this day we want to start studying the science of psychology. You will give yourself a better understanding of yourself and of other people through the study of psychology. Psychology is defined as the study of the mind and mental processes. You actually want to examine psychology, sociology, and human nature. It is wonderful to study these things, because sometimes we do things and wonder "Why?" We may wonder why someone we love behaves in a certain way. Having an understanding of psychology will give you an insight into some of these things. It will give you an idea of why certain things happen.

I'm not saying psychology is going to give you *all* of the answers, but it will definitely give you another way to look at things. When you understand people, and how they think, you will be able to experience greater success in business, in social settings, at your job, and in personal relationships.

There are many easy-to-read and enjoyable written and audio books on this subject. What I sometimes like to do on a Saturday afternoon is go to a new or used book store, or the public library, and browse the psychology section. I pick out four or five interesting titles from the shelf and preview them. I'll look at the layout, the table of contents, and the index. I'll usually read the introduction, pick a book that I like the most, and then buy or borrow it. What happens is, after reading that particular book I'll usually find something that they've referred me to— maybe another author, another book, or a CD set. So then I'll go back to the store or library and research that publication. This is a great way to find books on any subject and expand your knowledge. Although, I'm very grateful for my education, I'm a firm believer that you don't necessarily have to go to college to become an expert on a subject.

As your knowledge of psychology grows, you will also find your self-awareness increasing.

DAY 15 ACTION STEP

Set a date right now to obtain a publication about the subject of psychology. Take action right now—pull out your calendar, PDA, or your phone, then set a time and date to visit your public library or bookstore, to browse their psychology section. When you come back with the book or CD you have found interesting, write the title down here in this book. Set a goal of finishing the book within a reasonable amount of time that fits your schedule. Grow your list as time goes on.

DAY 16
<u>VOLUNTEER</u>

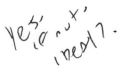

You will find many ways to volunteer if you're open to the experience. You can find a cause that you would like to support and work with a group consistently, or you can volunteer intermittently. "Why volunteer?" For many reasons; for one it is a great way to make a contribution to society. It is also a wonderful way to learn new things, and you may meet some interesting people while you're volunteering. It also just makes you feel good to add value to a positive cause!

Volunteering makes me feel good because I am able to share my most valuable asset: time. It is nice to give money; it is also great to give other resources that are of value to you. When you can share your time, you're sharing the ultimate gift. Unlike money, time can't be earned back; that's what makes volunteer work such a special offering to those in need.

If you have a unique or sought-after profession or skill, donate your professional services to a group in need. Set up a schedule that works for you. Maybe one day out of a month you can donate your time providing your services to an organization or to individuals that need the help. Do whatever works for you; just find a way to volunteer in some capacity.

<u>DAY 16 ACTION STEP</u>

Grab a pen and write three or more ways that you can enjoy volunteering. I'm not saying that you need to do all three, but come up with several ways of volunteering that may be interesting to you. It could be on a project by project basis, or it could be on a short/long-term basis. If it is a charitable organization that you would like to be more involved with, you could volunteer to be on the board. If you're an officer for the organization, that's also considered volunteering because you're not getting paid.

_____

_____

_____

_____

_____

_____

_____

_____

www.MondaySmiles.com

DAY 17
ELIMINATE EXCUSES

It's time to eliminate excuses from your life. Many of us have been using them as a crutch for way too long. There is a great, short poem that I learned when I was pledging my fraternity, Omega Psi Phi. It sums up the uselessness of excuses in the best way that I have ever heard.

<u>Excuses</u>

What are excuses?

Excuses are monuments of nothingness,

Which build bridges to nowhere,

And those who use those tools of incompetence,

Are Masters of Nothingness.

I love this poem, because I don't ever want to be a Master of Nothingness. Eliminate excuses and speak in solutions. Instead of talking about why something didn't work, figure out ways to *make* it work.

Once again, once you see what doesn't work, you're one step closer to finding out what does work.

DAY 17 ACTION STEP

Every time you catch yourself making an excuse, ask yourself these questions:

143

1. What are some solutions?
2. How can I fix this?
3. What can I do to make the situation better?
4. How can I take responsibility for my actions?

By asking those questions, you are taking responsibility. Especially if you're taking actions and speaking in a solution-oriented fashion.

_____

_____

_____

_____

_____

_____

_____

_____

_____

_____

DAY 18
PRACTICE EXCELLENCE

The way I practice excellence is quite simple. I continually ask myself this question:

"AM I DOING MY BEST?"

If the answer is yes, then I am practicing excellence. If the answer is no, then I ask myself two questions:

1. Why am I not doing my best?

2. How can I start doing my best right now, right where I am?

By practicing excellence you are increasing your own self-awareness and pushing yourself to your limits. The more you practice this technique, the more you'll practice excellence, and the sooner it will become a habit.

Now, does that mean that by practicing excellence you are going to get it right the first time? Of course not. Does it mean that you won't fail? Of course not. What it means in basic terms is that you'll maintain an "excellent state of mind." You will continue to persist and excel in the face of difficulty, and you will know that you are doing the best that you are capable of doing at this given moment in time.

<u>DAY 18 ACTION STEP</u>

It's action time. Write at least three ways that you will remind yourself to practice excellence. Some ideas are:

1. Write notes and put them in certain places where you will look at them regularly and remind yourself.
2. Carry a charm, a rock, a medallion, or any little object. Any time you touch the object, it will remind you of this particular exercise.
3. Create an email or calendar alarm.
4. Partner with a friend to help keep you accountable for your excellence. Maybe you can meet up and check in with this friend, every Monday or Friday with a phone call or a face-to-face meeting.

Whatever your preference may be, find a foolproof way to remind yourself to practice excellence every day of the year. Decide on your three possible methods now.

_____

_____

_____

_____

_____

www.MondaySmiles.com

DAY 19
BE A STAR AND
LET YOUR LIGHT SHINE

It's time to start allowing the inner you to shine through in your everyday interactions.

Most of us stifle our true selves for several reasons; one of them being the fear of rejection, which is basically the fear of not being liked or accepted. Another inhibitor is the fear of our own greatness. This chapter will be served by a quote, which I keep on my wall, by Marianne Williamson:

"Our worse fear is not that we are inadequate.
Our deepest fear is that we are powerful beyond measure.
It is our light not our darkness that most frightens us.
We ask ourselves,
Who am I not to be brilliant, gorgeous, talented, fabulous?
Actually, who are you not to be?
You are a child of God.
Your playing small does not serve the world.
There is nothing enlightening about shrinking so that other
people won't feel insecure around you.
We are meant to shine, as children do.
We were born to make manifest the glory of God within us.
It is not just in some of us; it is in everyone.
And as we let our own light shine, we unconsciously give
other people permission to do the same.

As we are liberated from our own fear,
Our presences automatically liberates others."

I love that poem. When I catch myself stifling myself, I think about it and release the inhibition. Or sometimes I even sing a little fitting verse of a song that many of us may have heard before.

"This little light of mine, I'm gonna let it shine. Let it shine, let it shine, let it shine."

Let your light shine.

DAY 19 ACTION STEP

Write down at least one way that you will allow your inner light to shine.

How can you step outside of the box? How can you be true, or better yet, *more* true to your inner star? It doesn't have anything to do with being an entertainer or performer of some sort. This can be something like being a better parent, being a better student, being a better teacher, or even being a mentor to someone. You can find ways unique to your own lifestyle and situation that will allow your own light to shine. Whatever you decide, let it shine, let it shine, let it shine.

_____

_____

_____

_____

_____

_____

_____

_____

_____

_____

_____

_____

_____

_____

www.MondaySmiles.com

DAY 20
TAKE PHOTOS OF THINGS
THAT YOU FIND BEAUTIFUL

Here is a fun and simple way to increase your happiness and heighten your perception of what is around you. Take photos of things that you find beautiful. Taking photos of beautiful things helps you to start *looking* for the things that you find beautiful. It increases your awareness of and appreciation for the beauty that surrounds you.

The great thing about taking photos is that you can put them in a photo box, a photo album, or hang them around your home or office. Your album will grow over time, and you can always go back and look at it when you need an injection of beauty in your day. It will always remind you of those things that you find beautiful, which can sometimes put you in a better state.

DAY 20 ACTION STEP

You may have a digital camera; maybe one on your cell phone. If not, you can just purchase an inexpensive camera or even a disposable one. Set a date to have your first photo shoot. Develop or print the photos, review them, allow the images to enhance your mood, and remind yourself of the things that you find beautiful.

---

www.MondaySmiles.com

DAY 21
SURROUND YOURSELF WITH
A VARIETY OF PEOPLE

Surround yourself with people who enrich your life. Invest your time with a variety of people from different backgrounds, age groups, races, and religions. Why? Because they all offer different perspectives that will add to your life experience.

This planet is filled with some very interesting people. Don't deprive yourself of their company! You don't want to limit yourself by only hanging around people who are just like you — what are you learning from people who have your same experience? Expand your horizons by learning about different people and different cultures. Experience the varying cultures of people from the inside. Take a genuine interest in people and where they are from, try different foods, and learn about different customs and traditions. Go to special art fairs, world music concerts, yoga studios, dance classes, foreign film festivals, and other events that you wouldn't normally attend. Be creative; surround yourself with positive people who want to grow and expand their vision as well.

DAY 21 ACTION STEP

Locate three or more activities that are happening in your area within the next 90 days. These should be events that you would have never even thought about attending in the past. Explore something that is off your normal path. Go to the events and be open for the experience. Enjoy yourself. Most importantly, be open to meeting new people and learning from them.

_____

_____

_____

_____

_____

_____

_____

_____

_____

_____

_____

_____

DAY 22
SEND A KIND NOTE
OR CARD TO A FRIEND,
FAMILY MEMBER OR ASSOCIATE

I learned this from one of my sisters. It's a wonderful feeling to receive a kind note or a simple card in the mail from someone you care about. To me, it seems even more special when it is for no particular reason at all, meaning it's not your birthday or a holiday. It means someone took the time out of their day to think about you and take a physical action on those thoughts. You can give that same feeling to others and it's a great investment in a relationship that usually has positive effects for all parties involved.

So, take a moment every now and then and send a kind note to a friend, family member, or an associate. You can also do this on a regular basis—whatever suits you. It will make their day, and probably yours too.

DAY 22 ACTION STEP

Write down the names of at least three people who you will send a handwritten note to. Send one note or card to each one of those people on your list within the next 24 hours. You will be brightening the day of three people. Grow your list as time goes on.

_____

_____

_____

_____

_____

_____

_____

_____

_____

_____

_____

_____

_____

_____

DAY 23
<u>REWARD YOURSELF FOR YOUR</u> <u>ACHIEVEMENTS & CELEBRATE THE WINS—</u> <u>BOTH SMALL & LARGE</u>

Sometimes we set goals for ourselves and achieve them. Then, before we even have a chance to think about it, we're off to accomplish our next goal without ever taking a moment to relish the victory.

Now I do agree that once you see yourself getting close to one goal, you should look ahead to set your next one. But while that is important, it is also important to take a moment to really enjoy and reflect on the things that you have accomplished thus far.

When you create a goal, also create a reward to go along with it. Treat yourself to a movie or buy your favorite CD. If you decide that after you save 10% of your income, you're going to spend 1% on something else that you like, then excellent, do that. If you study for one straight hour, then at the beginning of the next hour reward yourself with a ten minute break. Once you get down to a size 10 or whatever your weight goal is, then go out and buy yourself a new blouse, skirt, or pants. It doesn't matter what the reward is, as long as it is something productive that you like or enjoy. This will make the work a lot more enjoyable and increase your goal-achieving strength.

<u>DAY 23 ACTION STEP</u>

In your journal, write at least three things that you will reward yourself with as soon as you make certain steps towards your goal.

Suggestions:

- A new pair of shoes
- A vacation
- A day off
- A leisurely hour in the park reading a good book
- A dinner out with some friends to celebrate

DAY 24

SET AN EXAMPLE

Many people don't realize that sometimes the only way to make a positive change in others is to set an example for them to follow. Before taking an action, first take a moment to be aware that someone is always watching you. Therefore you can always make an effort to set the best example possible. This also another form of self-leadership.

Another idea which is kind of fun is to play a mental game with yourself. For this game you are going to believe that whatever you do at any given moment is going to go down in history forever. People are going to follow your example from this one action for years to come. Think about how your grandchildren or your great grandchildren will learn about all the things that you did and how they are going to do them exactly the way that you're going to do them. Even if you are absolutely sure that no one is watching, you can pretend that someone is taking notes on how to be the best human being possible by watching you. Do what you're capable of doing, but if you truly know that you're doing your very best in every moment, you can feel great about the example that you're setting.

DAY 24 ACTION STEP

Write down three ways that you can begin to practice setting a positive example right now. It could be at work, in social settings, or in your personal life.

DAY 25
BANISH COMPLAINTS

Banish complaints from your life! They are useless. What purpose does complaining serve? I'm not sure what good everyday mumbling and grumbling does; I honestly don't think that there is any productive purpose in complaining. It makes everyone around you miserable, and while you may think it will make you feel better, it actually just puts you into a bad, unproductive state.

Now, I'm not talking about taking the time to register a proper complaint when you receive poor service. I'm talking about when you complain about any and everything to any and everyone that will listen.

Rather than complain, think of solutions. How can you make the problem go away while skipping the urge to grumble about it? Again, speak in solutions and you will use your mind in positive and productive ways.

DAY 25 ACTION STEP

For the next three to twenty one days, each time you catch yourself complaining about anything or anyone, write down your complaint. Then put one line through it to cross it out. Rephrase what you complained about in a positive, productive, solution-oriented manner. Write down your modified statement. You'll find yourself taking more and more responsibility for your thoughts and emotions.

For example, instead of saying... "That jerk cut me off in traffic," cross that out and try something more productive like, "He's probably dealing with an emergency right now, and thank goodness neither one of us was hurt." You'll find that when you rephrase your complaints in this way, you will maintain your positive state and also become more understanding of others.

_____

_____

_____

_____

_____

_____

_____

_____

_____

_____

_____

_____

_____

_____

_____

_____

_____

_____

_____

_____

_____

_____

_____

www.MondaySmiles.com

DAY 26
MAKE A LIST OF WHO
OR WHAT YOU LOVE

Here is a simple action you can take towards achieving a pure and unconditional happiness. Make a list of whom or what you love. Sometimes it's enough to simply make a list about those you love. This list can include any person, place, or thing that you feel strongly about. These feelings of love put you in a wonderful state. Listing your loved ones (or things) is a simple and straightforward way to experience a jolt of happiness.

DAY 26 ACTION STEP

Start your own ongoing list of whom or what you love. Allow it to grow and you will see how your heart will fill from the happiness growing within. Refer to this "love list" regularly.

_____

_____

_____

_____

www.MondaySmiles.com

_____

_____

_____

_____

_____

_____

_____

_____

_____

_____

_____

_____

_____

_____

DAY 27
TREAT LIFE AS A GAME AND
HAVE FUN PLAYING IT...

Very simply, sometimes we take life way too seriously. It would be a good idea to actually *enjoy* the game of life. Find ways to turn problems into puzzles, and work into productive play. Be creative and use your imagination.

Examples:

1. As stated earlier, turn cleaning your house into an exercise routine.

2. Turn sitting in traffic into a game of a test of your patience and serenity.

3. Turn cleaning your garage into a treasure or "EBay" hunt.

4. When talking to your spouse or friend about the issues you may have had during the workday, talk in terms of challenges and find the fun in creating solutions.

5. When things happen that may seem bad at the time, search for productive reasons as to why they could have happened. Spin the situation into something that can help you in some way.

<u>DAY 27 ACTION STEP</u>

What three chores or problems can you turn into a game? Don't just think about them, write them down right now!

_____

_____

_____

_____

_____

_____

_____

_____

_____

_____

_____

www.MondaySmiles.com

DAY 28
CLEAR THE CLUTTER FROM YOUR LIFE

Make it a point to go through your closets at least every six months to a year and donate all of your old clothes, shoes, or whatever it is that you find that you're not using or don't plan to use, and give them to an organization of your choice. Be honest with yourself; generally, if you haven't used it in the past six months you probably don't need it. If you don't plan to ever use it, give it to someone who can. Otherwise, you're just wasting space.

Now this does several things. First of all, you're helping out someone who is probably less fortunate than yourself, and that may make you feel good. Secondly, you're clearing out the clutter and exercising your ability to let things go. Thirdly, you're creating a vacuum and a space for newer and better things for yourself. Donating your old or infrequently used clothing and items is a great way to give and receive at the same time. You're making a contribution and receiving good feelings (and possibly new things) in return.

DAY 28 ACTION STEP

Mission: Banish the pack-rat. Set a date right now to go through your closets and other storage spaces, and begin to let go. Let go of the things that you're not using or don't plan to use. Once you decide that you're going to

166

let the items go, do so immediately. Don't just fill a bag or a box and leave it by the door; move them from your space completely. You'll also be moving them from your mind.

DAY 29
<u>BE UNCOMFORTABLE,</u>
<u>STRETCH YOURSELF</u>

Find ways to move out of your comfort zone. Create ways to stretch yourself.

In order to build muscles you must push yourself to the limit, rest... and recover. Push yourself to the limit...rest...then recover. Then push yourself to the limit...rest...then recover again.

Of course, having the proper nutrition and techniques in place are important factors as well. The more you push, then push some more, the stronger your muscles will become, and the more your limits increase. The more you push, the more you'll able to push further. Your capacity increases and your muscles grow.

The same techniques used to build your body can be used to build your mind. Use these same techniques when learning to play a new instrument or learning to speak a new language. When you do the things that you're uncomfortable doing, you're pushing yourself to the limit and increasing your capacity. Do things that you know will help you grow as a person.

Why do this? To stay out of a rut. A rut can also be referred to as a shallow grave. It has been said; if you're not growing then you're dying. So live, make mistakes, and don't be afraid to look silly.

Once you're playing that new instrument or speaking that new language, then you've expanded your world a bit and are continuing to grow. You will have changed your perspective and added new experiences to your life.

Examples:

1. Take a public speaking class or join Toastmasters. If you're afraid to speak in front of people, that is even more reason to do this. Conquer that fear.
2. Make a pact to meet at least three new people at every party or networking event that you attend.
3. Learn a new language.
4. Travel to a non-English speaking country.
5. Volunteer for a leadership role on a project at work.
6. Ask a pertinent question in a group setting.
7. Pick up a new hobby.
8. Take a class in something that you're interested in, but that you feel will challenge you.
9. Increase your vocabulary.
10. Read challenging publications (with a dictionary by your side if necessary).

DAY 29 ACTION STEP

Write three ways in which you will choose to push your envelope, stretch yourself, and do a bit more than you normally would. Treat life like the adventure it was meant to be!

_____

_____

_____

_____

_____

_____

_____

_____

_____

_____

_____

_____

www.MondaySmiles.com

DAY 30
FIGURE OUT WAYS TO CHEER UP
A FRIEND IF THEY NEED IT....

Day 30! Wow! We made it...congratulations!!!

We are probably in agreement by now that happiness comes from the inside. I think that one of the greatest things you can do on earth is help someone find their own joy; in other words, what makes them intrinsically happy.

Of course, you can't do this without their consent or willing participation, but you can act as a catalyst to jump-start or temporarily change someone's emotional state. This will help to get the ball rolling for them so that they can move into a place of choosing happiness on their own. That's what day 30 is all about: figuring out ways to cheer up a friend, family member, or associate if they need it.

So create a list of things that you can do to uplift a friend or cheer up a family member. This list can include anything from the usual kind acts of buying flowers, taking the person to dinner, taking a walk on the beach, or having a talk at the park. Sometimes the most valuable act that you can do for another is just lending them your ear.

How about taking the person hiking, watching their children play, playing some upbeat music, or perhaps even

171

taking that person to an upbeat exercise class. It's really hard to be in a down mood when you're exercising to upbeat music in a room full of people who are working on bettering themselves. (Side note: make sure that both of you are physically fit and have checked with a Medical Professional before taking on any new exercise or fitness program).

Once you've created this list, you can use it immediately to cheer up a friend, family member, or associate. Of course, in the process of helping them, you may also cheer yourself up!

DAY 30 ACTION STEP

Start your "cheer up" list today and add to it regularly. And don't just write about it...again, take action! Go down the list and perform each action for the people you have in mind.

_____

_____

_____

_____

_____

www.MondaySmiles.com

www.MondaySmiles.com

IT'S UP TO YOU

Now that I have given you the tools that I have found to be effective in choosing happiness… most of the time, it is now up to you to actually use this information to your benefit. This information will only benefit you if you actually implement it into your own life and situation.

So are you going to live a risk-free, play-it-safe life, or are you going to start on the road to a happy, courageous, passion-filled life? The choice is yours. No matter what you have gone through in life, you can achieve happiness, but it's 100% up to you. I have told you the intimate details of my life, and how I came to my success in life. If I would have sat around and felt sorry for myself, I would not have been able to achieve the happiness I enjoy today.

Make a conscious decision to stand up and take unadulterated, genuine happiness into your possession. You've made it this far, so I'm sure you can do it! Believe in yourself and do it now!

"Most folks are about as happy as they make up their minds to be…"

\- Abraham Lincoln

APPENDIX

Recommended Reading

Mega Living! by Robin Sharma

The Power of Awareness by Neville

Joy – The Happiness that Comes From Within by OSHO

You Can Be Happy No Matter What by Richard Carlson

You Can Have it All by Arnold M. Patent

Mind Power into the 21st Century by John Kehoe

Dynamic Thought by Henry Thomas Hamlin

The Power Mind System by Michael Monroe Kiefer

As a Man Thinketh by James Allen

Creative Visualization by Shakti Gawain

Excuse Me Your Life is Waiting by Lynn Grabhorn

The Magic of Believing by Claude Bristol

The Power of Your Subconscious Mind by Joseph Murphy

Psycho-cybernetics by Maxwell Maltz

Feel the Fear and Do it Anyway by Susan Jeffers

The Power of Now by Eckhart Tolle

Other Recommended Programs

Creative Ways to Choose Happiness by Chappale Linn Burton (DVD Program)

The Psychology of Achievement by Brian Tracy (Audio Program)

Live Your Dreams by Les Brown (Audio Program)

How to Choose Happiness...Most of the Time by Chappale Linn Burton (A truncated version of this book is also available in audio format).

About the Author
Chappale Linn Burton

At a very young age, Chappale Linn Burton witnessed the tragic murder of his step-father and biological mother while playing on the playground in his birthplace of Chicago, Illinois. He has not only forgiven the assailant, but has now dedicated his life to sharing tools and techniques that he used to overcome the negative effects that event *could* have had on his life. He is now a motivational speaker and coach who currently resides in Los Angeles, California. He has a degree in Psychology from the University of Pittsburgh in Pittsburgh, Pennsylvania.

His most notable accomplishments during his time at Pitt were walking onto the Division 1 track team, earning an athletic scholarship, and becoming the most valuable player (MVP) and team captain by his senior year. Chappale started his professional career as a milieu therapist for one of the leading psychiatric hospitals in

Pittsburgh before moving on to help people further in his roles as a personal trainer, coach, HR manager and executive recruiter.

He has been a student and teacher of self-development principles for the past twenty years, and has helped (and continues to help) many people to make positive choices in their day-to-day lives.

You may also benefit from some of the experiences that Chappale shares in his recently released DVD, *Creative Ways to Choose Happiness,* which was recorded in front of a live audience.

Give this book as a gift!

HOW TO CHOOSE HAPPINESS...
MOST OF THE TIME
BY CHAPPALE LINN BURTON

Check your Local Bookstore or Order Here

YES, I want _____ copies of *How to Choose Happiness... Most of the Time* at $19.99 each. FREE shipping and handling for orders of 10 or more books.

YES, I am a bookstore, distributor, or wholesaler interested in purchasing *How to Choose Happiness... Most of the Time* for our inventory. Please send me more information.

— · — · — · — · — · — · — · — · — · — · — · — · — · — · — · — · — · — · —

Please include $2.99 shipping and handling for one book, $1.50 for each additional book. California residents **must** include sales tax. Payment must accompany all orders. Allow 7-14 days for delivery.

My check or money order for $_____ is enclosed.
Please charge my __ Visa __ Mastercard __ American Express

Name _____

Organization_____

Address _____

City/State/Zip _____

Phone _____

E-mail _____

Card #_____ Exp. Date_____

Signature _____

(over)

Please call 818-920-4940

if you have any questions that have not
been answered on our website:

http://www.MondaySmiles.com

Monday Smiles, LLC
P.O. Box 480192
Los Angeles, CA 90048

Make your check or money order payable to
Monday Smiles, LLC and return with this form to:

Monday Smiles, LLC
P.O. Box 480192
Los Angeles, CA 90048

Allow 7 - 14 days for delivery.
Check your Local Bookstore, Online,
or Order Here

www.MondaySmiles.com
Your personal guide to choosing
success, growth and happiness.

Made in the USA
San Bernardino, CA
29 January 2020